THE SACRAMENTS: ENCOUNTERING THE RISEN LORD

THE SACRAMENTS: ENCOUNTERING THE RISEN LORD

REV. PAUL A. FEIDER

Ave Maria Press • Notre Dame, Indiana

The author has donated all royalties earned by the sale of this book to Mother Teresa of Calcutta and the Missionaries of Charity.

Scripture texts used in this work are taken from *The New American Bible* copyright © 1970 by the Confraternity of Christian Doctrine, Washington, D.C., and are used by permission of copyright owner. All rights reserved.

Cover design: Elizabeth J. French

Printed and bound in the United States of America.

TABLE OF CONTENTS

To Mother Teresa
who through her many
sacred, sacramental actions
enables the poor and the dying
to encounter the Risen Lord

INTRODUCTION

Jesus said,
"I solemnly assure you,
the man who has faith in me
will do the works I do
and greater far than these.
Why? Because I go to the Father,
and whatever you ask in my name
I will do,
so as to glorify the Father in the Son."
(John 14:12-13)

It is hard to know exactly what Jesus meant with those words to his apostles, but they seem to carry a mandate as well as a challenge. One way to reflect on that mandate is to consider which actions of Jesus need to be done again and again in order that "greater works" may be accomplished, that more people reap the benefits of his words and actions. Which actions did Jesus perform to lead those around him to greater fullness of life?

People were amazed at how Jesus' touch, his words, his encounters could be so transforming. They stood in awe at the life he transmitted through his personality.

We ask ourselves how can we in our ministry carry on his works? How can we as a church community do what he did to make his presence felt? How can we re-enact his gestures? How can we make his words and actions burst with the life-giving power of his love?

It is with these questions in mind that I would like to reflect on the sacred actions of Jesus which have come to be called *sacraments*. I find these reflections necessary since the sacraments within the Catholic church are surrounded with numerous misunderstandings and unan-

swered questions. People ask, What happens to babies if
they die before they are baptized? Do I have to be confirmed? Why do I have to tell my sins to a priest? Can't I
go right to the top? Why must I go to Mass? Why do I
have to go through preparation to get married? Why can't
priests get married? Do they still do the sacrament of Extreme Unction? and so on. Such questions indicate a serious need to understand the actions of Jesus that form the
roots of the sacraments.

Not only have the sacraments caused misunderstandings and questions in the Catholic community, but history
shows that sometimes these very actions of Jesus evolved
into gestures and rites that caused divisions among Christian communities. The church found itself doing things
that did not look anything like the gestures of Jesus. Some
sacraments were no longer seen as "instituted by Christ"
and they became sources of controversy and division.
Other sacramental actions were discarded completely.

In an attempt to answer questions and to clarify confusing and divisive misunderstandings, we will examine
the scriptural roots and the historical development of
what have come to be known as the seven sacraments of
the Roman Catholic Church, namely baptism, confirmation, eucharist, reconciliation, anointing of the sick, marriage, and holy orders. Such an examination is not easy to
make since the details of history are colored by time and
human limitations.

I am aware that in trying to show the historical development of the sacraments I will be making some as-
sumptions and accenting certain events from my perspective. All of recorded history is an interpretation of events.
I hope that the pieces of history I point out will help us
feel the church's challenge to keep alive the Spirit of Jesus
through his words and actions.

This little book, then, is my attempt to take you into
the past to examine the teachings and actions of Jesus in
order to discover how he led people to encounter the sav-

ing love of the Father. It is an attempt to walk back into history and experience the challenges of the early church as it sought to keep alive the memories and the saving power of the Lord. It is a journey into our Christian history to examine what influences hampered the church from carrying on the sacred actions of Jesus. It is a journey into the mystery of Jesus' life-giving presence left with his people in his words and actions.

We make this journey into history not only to answer questions or to clarify misunderstandings of the past, but also to help form a vision for the future, to continue seeking ways to re-enact the gestures of Jesus in meaningful expressions consistent with our roots. I write about the sacraments from the vision of a Catholic priest, for that is what the Lord has called me to be. I write as one who loves the church and seeks to enrich its mission. I write as one who has personally felt the power of celebrating the sacraments and have seen the transforming effects they can have on believing people. I pray that my efforts help in some way to open Catholics and all Christians to a deeper appreciation of these sacred actions.

ONE

Keeping the Fire Burning— The Sacraments

They said to one another, "Were not our hearts burning inside us as he talked to us on the road and explained the Scriptures to us?"

(Luke 24:32)

When we journey back to scriptural times, we find that the sacraments began as the early community's attempt to keep alive the *presence* of Jesus whom they loved. In one sense, the sacraments really began with the *absence* of Jesus. It is only after Jesus was physically absent that the community sought ways to make his presence felt, to keep the awareness of his love alive in their hearts, and to enable others to experience the beauty of a love so strong. Jesus had left them words and gestures which brought back memories of him after he had ascended to the Father. He had shown them how to express the Father's care and concern through words and actions. In these words and actions we find the roots of Christian sacraments.

As time went on, sacraments came to be defined as "outward signs, instituted by Christ, to give grace." By the year 1150 the church agreed upon seven such sacred signs or sacraments. The definition used by the church pointed out the essential parts of a sacrament. Each of these sacred actions includes an outward sign or symbolic gesture which Jesus made holy through his own attitudes and actions. Through these sacred actions his grace, his per-

11

sonal love is made available to his followers. This grace
flowing from the sacraments is not some kind of packaged
"stuff" that we receive, but rather it is the awareness of
the personal love of God. It is the life-giving power of
God's love which flows from celebrating, in expectant
faith, the actions that Jesus made holy. Jesus expressed his
love in these signs and we receive it to the extent that we
are open to being loved.

Like his sacred word preserved in the scriptures, the
sacraments are preservations of his attitudes and sacred
actions which convey his personal love for us. Perhaps another way to express it is to say that sacraments are actions
made holy by Jesus which enable us to experience his presence in our midst.

Sacraments are meant to help us *encounter* Jesus our
risen Lord through symbols and words. They originated
with Jesus' words and actions, but historically accumulated additional symbols and gestures which people found
helpful in making Jesus' presence felt. The sacraments are
constantly growing and developing. Through the sacraments we invite Jesus into our personal lives by celebrating with other Christians what we are, and what we hope
to become in him. It is a privilege to have people who will
celebrate these sacred mysteries with us.

As history developed, these sacred actions of Jesus
took on new forms, adapting to the culture and thought
patterns of the time. The actions became surrounded by
prayers and ceremonies. In some cases, the original gestures of Jesus were buried under rituals and ceremonies
very different from their beginnings. The Eucharist, for
example, became the adoration of a sacred object, an
action very different from the last supper. Reconciliation
became a place of judgment rather than an occasion to experience the abundant mercy of God. Jesus' healing gestures were lost almost completely in a sacrament that
came to be called Extreme Unction. Despite human errors
and outside influences, however, the church continued to

preserve in some form the power of God's presence in the sacraments.

Through much scriptural and historical research during this century and subsequent decisions made at the Second Vatican Council (1962-1965), the sacraments have been significantly restored to their original order and intent. Indeed, many of the ceremonies and rituals which accumulated around the sacraments throughout the middle centuries have been eliminated, leaving us sacraments that look more like the actions of Jesus, and convey his attitudes in a more powerful way. As we look at each sacrament individually, we will see when and why these changes came about, and perhaps come to appreciate the efforts of renewal involved.

In seeking to understand the roots and history of each sacrament, it seems important to realize that we are dealing in some way with the *mystery* of how God's love is expressed and received, therefore the effects of these encounters can never fully be discovered nor understood. The words and actions of Jesus convey his personality and his love, which have the power to change people's lives. Anytime the church repeats those words and actions as a community in faith, his love is present and something happens, no matter how well or poorly the action is carried out. A nervous fumbling through the rite of anointing results in the restoration of health. The words said to someone in the sacrament of reconciliation are exactly what they needed to hear.

Though God's power can be effective through simple words and imperfect celebrations, it is our constant challenge as church to seek ways of making the sacraments truly personal encounters with a God who cares. Our efforts toward this goal can bring greater numbers of people to experience the love that Jesus has for them, as well as his desire to be intimately involved in their lives.

BAPTISM AND CONFIRMATION

Historical Development

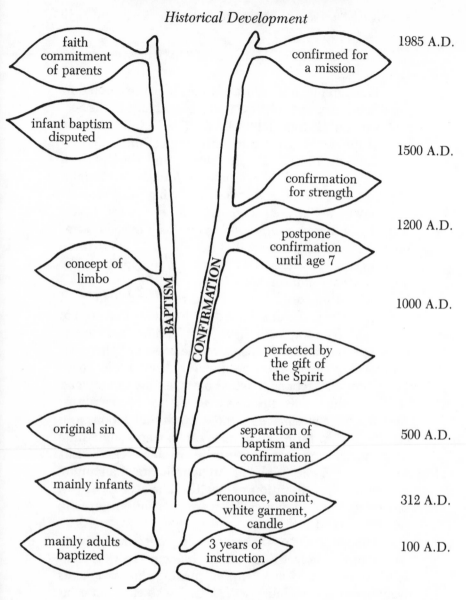

faith commitment of parents

infant baptism disputed

concept of limbo

original sin

mainly infants

mainly adults baptized

BAPTISM

CONFIRMATION

confirmed for a mission

confirmation for strength

postpone confirmation until age 7

perfected by the gift of the Spirit

separation of baptism and confirmation

renounce, anoint, white garment, candle

3 years of instruction

1985 A.D.

1500 A.D.

1200 A.D.

1000 A.D.

500 A.D.

312 A.D.

100 A.D.

Scriptural Roots

Acts 2:37-38 Reform and be baptized
John 14:16-17 Promise of the Spirit
John 20:19-20 Spirit of peace
Acts 2:1-4 Pentecost
Mark 1:10-11 Jesus' baptism
Luke 4:18-19 Spirit upon Jesus
Acts 8:36-39 Into the water
Romans 6:3-4 Buried with Christ

Acts 10:44-48 Baptism through listening
Acts 8:14-17 Laying on of Hands
Acts 19:3-6 Laying on of Hands
Matthew 28:19 Trinitarian formula
Romans 10:9 Profession of faith
Galatians 3:27 Clothed in Christ
Acts 16:33 Household baptized
John 3:3 Born from above

TWO

Bathing in the Holy Spirit — Baptism and Confirmation

When they heard this, they were deeply shaken. They asked Peter and the other apostles, "What are we to do, brothers?" Peter answered: "You must reform and be baptized, each one of you, in the name of Jesus Christ, that your sins may be forgiven; then you will receive the gift of the Holy Spirit."

(Acts 2:37-38)

Scriptural Roots

What are we to do? This is the question which impelled the early church from the first Pentecost to develop some ceremony of initiation into the community. They sought to help people experience the freedom of repentance and the welcoming love of God's Spirit. They had known from John the Baptist the powerful experience of turning their lives away from sin and being cleansed by the mercy of God symbolized by bathing in water. Even though John's baptism was a washing in preparation for the Messiah, the church could use that gesture of washing to symbolize people's turning from sin and opening to the Spirit promised by Jesus. It was a way of demonstrating or celebrating a person's change of lifestyle. We can see here the first roots of the sacrament of baptism and confirmation, which were celebrated as one event in the beginning of the church. Today, in most cases, they are celebrated as two complementary sacraments to help people experience the peace and strength of God's love in their lives.

In his words to his disciples before he died, Jesus promised to send the Holy Spirit that they might feel his presence remaining in them.

15

> "I will ask the Father
> and he will give you another
> Paraclete —
> to be with you always:
> the Spirit of truth. . ." (Jn 14:16-17).

After his resurrection these words came to fulfillment as
he anointed them with his Spirit of peace (Jn 20:19-20).
That Spirit is not fully encountered or accepted until the
day of Pentecost when the disciples are gathered in
prayer. We read in the Acts of the Apostles,

> Suddenly from up in the sky there came a noise
> like a strong, driving wind which was heard all
> through the house where they were seated.
> Tongues as of fire appeared, which parted and
> came to rest on each of them. All were filled
> with the Holy Spirit (Acts 2:2-4).

At that point the early disciples were baptized. They
were immersed in the living presence of their risen Lord
and formed into a unity of faith, ready to proclaim with
boldness the saving message of Jesus. There was no water
used, but the Spirit of God is not limited to the gesture of
immersing in water. Some of them may have been baptized in water with John's baptism of repentance, but here
they are simply immersed in the overwhelming love of
their Lord. What seems most significant is that the community was gathered together "devoting themselves to
constant prayer" (Acts 1:14). This attitude of openness to
the Spirit of God seems essential for the sacrament of baptism.

Once the first disciples experienced the Spirit of Jesus, they were impelled to share that experience with others. Even though they had not been immersed in water
for baptism, they saw the value of using water to enable
people to experience the cleansing and empowering Spirit
of their Lord. The action of immersing new Christians in
water became a powerful way of allowing them to feel

washed clean of the past and refreshed in the love of God.

Baptism by water may not have become so significant to the early church if Jesus himself had not been baptized. In accepting baptism, Jesus gave new meaning to the baptismal action, which had been used in various ways prior to his time as a gesture of purification. Jesus seems to have experienced the overwhelming love of the Father at this moment. St. Mark writes, "Immediately upon coming up out of the water he saw the sky rent in two and the Spirit descending on him like a dove. Then a voice came from the heavens: "You are my beloved Son. On you my favor rests" (Mk 1:10-11).

Shortly after his baptism, Jesus spoke of the Spirit of God being upon him when he began his public ministry in Nazareth. We read in Luke's gospel,

> "The Spirit of the Lord is upon me;
> therefore, he has anointed me.
> He has sent me to bring glad tidings to the
>   poor,
> to proclaim liberty to captives,
> recovery of sight to the blind
> and release to prisoners,
> to announce a year of favor from the Lord"
>   (Lk 4:18-19).

Here Jesus proclaimed the power of his baptismal experience. He connected the action of baptism with the coming of the Spirit, the realization of the Father's love. It seems that through that gesture of baptism and prayer, the Father anointed him with a deep awareness of his love and commissioned him to proclaim the good news of forgiveness and healing.

As the early church reflected on Jesus' baptism, they came to realize the power in the baptismal commitment symbolized by immersing in water. Since Jesus had connected that action with the affirmation of the Father's love, it seem appropriate for the early church to use that gesture to enable people entering the community to experience the Holy Spirit. It symbolized turning away from one's old lifestyle and being open to the Spirit directing the new life ahead.

I'm sure the early church wondered why Jesus, who was without sin, received this baptism of repentance. Gradually, it seems, the early Christians came to see in his baptism powerful symbolism, a symbol of his acceptance of baptism for the sins of all people. This makes us aware of the connection between Jesus' baptism and his passion and death. His commitment to the Father's will at baptism meant acceptance of the Father's will at the crucifixion. It may lead us to realize why the early church emphasized the dying to self, the letting go of their own will that was part of entering the death and resurrection of Jesus through baptism. It may also prod us to ponder what our baptism and confirmation has meant in our lives.

The scriptural roots show us a number of interesting facts about the sacraments of baptism and confirmation. In the Acts of the Apostles we read how baptism-confirmation involved a decision to repent of past sins before a person could enter the Christian community. Here Luke was speaking of adults who wish to become part of the community. This commitment to change and live by the values of Jesus was emphasized in the early years of the church. It was so stressed that if someone committed a serious public sin after turning their life to God through baptism, the church did not know how to treat that person. Gradually the sacrament of reconciliation developed to deal with post-baptismal sins.

This emphasis on repentance and forgiveness of sins seemed out of place as the sacrament of baptism came to be administered to infants. We will see the historical development how this adaptation became a source of many questions. Gradually it became evident that infants do not need to have sinned before they can be bathed in the Spirit of God through baptism. This does not mean that baptism for infants has no effect. Celebrated in faith, baptism frees an infant from the darkness or effects of sin.

Miraculous healings have occurred through the baptism of seriously ill infants in the hospital as the Spirit of God freed them from the power of darkness.

The idea of making a commitment to Jesus Christ as Lord was also hard to adapt to children being baptized. At that time the focus moved to the parents and sponsors who spoke for the child. In recent times, the sacrament of confirmation is being received by young adults, which allows the candidates the opportunity to experience this early aspect of Christian initiation. These young adults are being challenged to choose personally to commit their lives to Jesus and the Christian community. The community is challenged to support this decision with prayers and good example.

We do not know exactly how the early baptism-confirmation sacrament was celebrated. It seems to have been done either by total immersion in water or by standing in water with the minister of the sacrament pouring water over the candidate's head. To "baptize" means to dip, to wash, or to immerse. The Acts of the Apostles (8:36-39) speaks of Philip taking the eunuch "down into the water" to be baptized, and coming "out of the water" with him, but it does not say exactly how he performed the baptism. The letter to the Hebrews (10:22) refers to Christians being "washed in pure water," but again it does not say how. St. Paul in his letter to the Romans (6:3-4) speaks about baptism as being "buried with Christ," but he does not state what form such a symbolic burial takes. Early Christian art pictures people standing in water waist deep for baptism while water is being poured over their heads. Whatever method of baptism is used, it is a symbol of immersing people in the Holy Spirit as they die to themselves and accept Jesus as their Lord.

It is also recorded in the Acts of the Apostles that the Spirit sometimes came upon people before they came to the baptismal water. In Acts 10:44-48, for example, we read that "the Holy Spirit descended upon all who were listening to Peter's message" before he had a chance to baptize them. Later Peter remarks, "What can stop these people who have received the Holy Spirit even as we have, from being baptized with water?" This indicates to us that sacramental actions do not limit the power of God's Spirit. In this case the baptism was a celebration of what already happened. At other times it was an opportunity to help someone experience the power of God's Spirit. Baptism and confirmation are not magical actions, but rather occasions to experience the mystery of Jesus' death and resurrection taking place within those who are making a commitment to him.

It is interesting that in a number of cases the laying on of hands seems to foster the experience of the Holy Spirit. In the Acts of the Apostles (8:14-17 and 19:5-6) the power of the Holy Spirit is reported to be transmitted through the laying on of hands by the apostles. These passages indicate why the laying on of hands has always in some way been associated with the initiation sacraments, and remains part of the sacrament of confirmation in the present day.

From earliest times, baptisms were done "in the name of the Father, and of the Son, and of the Holy Spirit" (Mt 28:19) in accordance with Jesus' commission as recorded at the end of Matthew's gospel. The references to being baptized in the "name of Jesus" only (Acts 2:38; 8:16; 10:48) seem to mean that candidates were baptized by the authority of Jesus. Again, no matter what the exact words, the desire to submit to the Lordship of Jesus, the openness to his Spirit, and commitment to the Christian community were the essential parts of the initiation sacrament in the beginning.

With this understanding we can see why the profession of one's faith in the Father, Son, and Holy Spirit was a central part of this sacrament. In his letter to the Romans (10:9) St. Paul indicates how important it is to profess our faith as part of the baptismal commitment. Earlier in this letter he defines the profession of faith and commitment as necessitating a "dying to sin." These references point out how much the early church stressed the candidates' decision to change from their old lifestyle to follow the lifestyle of Jesus.

In his letter to the Galatians (3:27) St. Paul refers to every Christian being "clothed with Christ" through baptism. This reference gave rise to the use of a white garment in the sacrament of baptism. Gradually an anointing with oil was added to symbolize identity with Christ, a name which means the anointed one. A lighted candle was also added to the ceremony indicating the coming of Christ to the newly baptized person. Each symbol is in some way rooted in scripture and is meant to help the candidate experience the life-giving love of the Lord.

There are a few references in the New Testament to whole households being baptized (Jn 4:53; Acts 16:33). I point this out because as history developed, the practice of baptizing infants became more prevalent. It seemed natural and acceptable from earliest times that when the parents were part of the community, the children were also received as members. In such cases, parents and sponsors spoke for the infants.

All of these scriptural roots add some dimension to the sacraments of baptism and confirmation. They show us how the actions and symbols of these sacraments developed, illustrating that the Holy Spirit was never limited to one action or event. When people ask, "Does a person have to be baptized in order to be saved?" we might well wonder if we can confine the saving love of God to one form or ritual. Jesus does tell us, according to John's gospel (3:3), that we must be "born from above" in order to enter the kingdom, but those words assume that a person has the opportunity to know him. It seems presumptuous of us Christians to think that the ceremony of baptism, as we know it, is the *only* way for Jesus' saving love to affect his people. Could there not be many ways for people to be "born from above," to let Jesus' saving grace affect their life decisions? Even those who do not know him can experience his love and live by his teachings. As Christians we are *privileged* to know him. We are privileged to have his life example to follow and to have the assurance that he walks with us through life. We are also privileged to have people in our lives who care enough to bathe us in the baptismal waters of Jesus' love. These sacraments are gifts to us and we are commissioned by Jesus to share them with others.

As history developed, some of these scriptural roots were emphasized more than others. The actions of the ceremony were adapted to some extent to particular times and cultures. Outside influences also altered the gestures, but through it all, the Spirit of God remained. That is the mystery of God's presence among his people.

Historical Development

It was a challenge for the early disciples to continue to help new Christians experience the saving love of Jesus in the way that they had experienced his presence. The memories of what his presence, his words, and his love did to them faded as the second and third generations of Christians entered the community.

The scanty bits of history from the first centuries indicate that gradually a form of Christian initiation developed which focused mainly on adults. Records from the third century tell us that candidates wishing to enter the community were brought to the community teacher and presented for acceptance into the church. The sponsors had to testify personally to the goodness of the candidates and their sincere desire to become Christians. The community was particular about whom it accepted, since the good example of the members' lives was their primary way of showing what Jesus was like or explaining the message he had proclaimed. Community witness was their most powerful tool for spreading the gospel.

Once accepted as candidates for baptism, the people went through a three-year instruction period called the catechumenate, learning about Jesus and the roots of the community. During this time the candidates attended the first part of the celebration of the Eucharist, but had to leave before the prayer of the faithful.

The community, and particularly the sponsors, lent encouragement and prayful support to the candidates. Today we are seeing a return to this kind of community and sponsor support as adults are being received into the church.

On Holy Saturday the candidates who had completed their instructions were baptized and confirmed in one welcoming event. For 40 days previous, they would have fasted and prayed. The community joined them in this time of fasting and prayer, which is the origin of the season of Lent. The final phase of the preparation involved an examination of the candidates' readiness for admission into the Christian community. Prayers of exorcism were prayed to cast out any forces of evil or sin that may have affected them as they lived in their non-Christian environment. Baptism was then celebrated with a three-fold immersing or pouring of water after the candidate answered "yes" to the three-fold profession of faith in the Father, the Son, and the Holy Spirit. It was not until the eighth century that the church started using the formula, "I baptize you in the name..." This is the form still being used today.

During the fourth century, other ceremonies and actions were added to the celebration of baptism-confirmation. First, the candidates stood on one side of the baptismal water and renounced Satan three times. After removing their clothes as a symbol of leaving their old lives behind, they would be anointed with the oil of catechumens. Next, they walked down into the water and received the three-fold immersion or pouring of water. As the newly baptized walked out of the water on the other side, they were clothed in a white garment as a sign of putting on the new life in Christ. Also at this time in history, baptismal candidates began to receive a lighted candle. Following this ceremony, the newly baptized were anointed with oil on the five senses by the bishop. This anointing by the bishop gradually developed into the sacrament of confirmation.

It is interesting that for a number of centuries the newly baptized were also offered a drink of milk and honey. This gesture seems to have symbolized receiving the fruits of God's blessings.

The initiation ceremony at this time in history captured the sense of commitment to Jesus and the community, as well as the bathing in God's Spirit. The community participated by fasting and by bringing the newly baptized into the celebration of the Eucharist after the baptism. Eucharist was always considered one of the initiation sacraments because it was the final sign that the people were full members of the church. Through the whole event, they could feel bathed in the love of God and the community. They could experience the risen presence of Jesus as they committed their lives to him.

Christian history indicates that from earliest times some infants received this sacrament. Gradually more and more children were being baptized and by the fourth century infant baptism became the norm. This transfer to infants of ceremonies designed for adults was impossible without alterations and some loss of meaning. The questions usually addressed to the candidate were now addressed to the parents and sponsors who answered for the infant. Instead of being received into the catechumenate for instruction, the child was simply welcomed with the Sign of the Cross on the forehead. The prayer of exorcism was prayed while imposing hands on the child, followed by the sprinkling of salt on the tongue. The infant, held by the sponsor, then was anointed and immersed three times in the water. This complete immersion for infants seems to have continued until the thirteenth century. A white garment was placed on the child and a lighted candle was presented to the parents. The reception of the Eucharist by the infant completed the initiation ceremonies. All of the words and symbols took on different meanings as these sacraments were adapted to infants. They continued to convey, however, the love of God and of the community.

The anointing following the immersion in water continued to be administered by the bishop, although by the fourth century, it was normally seen as a distinct rite from baptism, and usually included a laying on of hands. Already by the third century there was evidence of a second rite separate from, yet complementary to, baptism. We might understand why this separate rite became the norm, if we realize the history of the time. Christianity was no longer outlawed by the Romans, but became the official religion of the Roman Empire. This dramatic change in the legal standing of Christianity caused an influx of people joining the church and it made baptism necessary on many days of the year in various places. Because the bishop could not be present for all these baptisms, this anointing and laying on of hands was frequently celebrated later as a separate ceremony. By the ninth century other prayers and rituals were added to this rite which came to be called confirmation.

Since this separation of baptism and confirmation was first regarded as abnormal and less than ideal, the two events were celebrated as close together as possible. With time it seems people came to see value in confirmation being celebrated later, since by the 13th century it was postponed until age seven, and eventually, until age twelve. At present the age of seventeen or eighteen is becoming common. Through this separate sacrament of confirmation, the Christian was said to be completed or perfected by the gift of the Holy Spirit.

The action of anointing in confirmation symbolized

the person's identity with Christ the anointed one. The laying on of hands, when used, seemed to convey a sense of being enspirited for the Christian mission. The sign of peace, which at one point was expressed as a caress on the cheek (later it came to be a tap on the cheek), was meant to welcome the person into the community.

Infant baptism and confirmation had become the normal practice. It was a beautiful expression of love and concern by parents who wished their children to share in their gift of faith. This practice, however, came to be considered an immediate necessity due to the influence of non-Christian teachings and the church's response to them. In an effort to quiet the Pelagian heresy, and influenced by Manichean philosophy, St. Augustine taught that every child was born in sin. He was influenced by the belief that the sex act, even within marriage, was sinful. He believed that every child was marred by this "necessary sin," which was an effect of the original sin affecting the whole human race. In order to be saved from the effects of original sin, Augustine taught that every child had to be baptized immediately after birth lest they die and go to hell.

This teaching helped squelch the Pelagian heresy, which perpetuated the idea that people could save themselves, but it left many Christian parents concerned over the question, What if my baby dies before it is baptized? Until this time it was believed that such a child would be taken to the Lord on the basis of God's freeing love and the parents' desire to have their child in union with the Lord.

After this understanding of original sin became prevalent, however, the church could no longer assure parents that their children would have a place in heaven should they die before baptism. The church as a whole did not accept Augustine's theory that unbaptized babies would go to hell, but it did not know exactly where they went. To answer this dilemma, the church began to teach that unbaptized babies went to a place of "purely natural happiness" which came to be called Limbo. It was always nebulous as to what that meant and why such children could not be with the Lord.

It is only since the Second Vatican Council that the church has dispelled this misguided teaching and returned to the original understanding that unbaptized infants are safe in God's eternal presence. Contemporary theologians no longer understand original sin as a "black mark" on the infant's soul, but rather as a lack of grace because of being human and as the sin-filled environment into which every child is born. This teaching is in keeping with scripture and seems to fit more with the loving nature of God. It still makes us aware of the need to surround children in the love and guidance of the Holy Spirit through baptism to protect them from being overpowered by the effects of human sinfulness. This understanding still points to the need for Jesus' saving grace, and the privilege of having people who help us experience the freeing power of that grace. Baptism understood in this way is seen more as a filling with the Holy Spirit, rather than a washing off of sin.

In light of this new understanding, we see why the church stresses the need for parents and sponsors of a baptismal candidate to be practicing members of the church, adequately informed about their faith. They will be the ones responsible, together with the support of the community, to keep surrounding the child with the awareness of God's personal love. Infant baptism, as we saw in the scriptures and the early church, had meaning only if the parents were members of the community. Then it is a natural expression of the parents' love for their children. It is a sign of immersing them in God's love and guiding them with the teachings of Jesus.

By the fifth century, then, the church had two celebrations for an infant to be immersed in the love of the community and the power of the Holy Spirit. However, it no longer had a sacramental action for adults to experience the powerful presence of the Spirit that flows from making a commitment to the Lord. Baptism and confirmation remained pretty much through history from this point on sacraments for the very young. Perhaps that is why some of the reformers in the Middle Ages raised some questions about infant baptism, and wondered how adults might experience the filling with the Holy Spirit. Could this also be why in recent times the age of confirmation has been postponed until young adulthood?

Even though, as mentioned above, there is no separate rite of confirmation in the scriptures, it seems appropriate to have an occasion when people baptized as infants can confirm their faith in the Lord, and experience a fresh release of his Spirit. The two sacraments are meant to complement each other in enabling a person to experience the fullness of the gift of God's Spirit. Confirmation completes the initiation process begun at baptism, making the person a full member of the church.

The rite of confirmation, as renewed by Vatican II, has given new meaning to some of the actions of the early church initiation rites, such as the period of instruction, the sponsor's role, and the community prayers and support. The Rite of Christian Initiation for Adults, recently reinstated, is patterned almost exclusively on the early church's form of baptism-confirmation. Both of these rites celebrated with youths and adults challenge people to make a personal commitment to the Lord, and allow them to experience the power of God's Spirit flowing from that commitment.

In recent time, though the charismatic renewal within the Catholic church, as well as through sacramental renewal, many adults have more fully experienced what their baptism and confirmation symbolized. Through instruction in the Lord's love and the prayers of other Christians, many have come to experience a fresh release of the Holy Spirit, with a new awareness of the gifts of the Spirit. As we noted before, the Spirit of God is not limited by any one action, but responds to a person's decision to accept his love and live according to his words.

There is great hope for the church as it encourages its members to accept the personal love of Jesus for them, and to live in the awareness of that love. Whatever sacramental actions we can use to enable one another to experience that love as adults will enrich our lives and the lives of our communities. This is exactly what the early church was challenged to do after Jesus was gone. When they did these things, the church grew, and the risen presence of Jesus was encountered in their midst. That is our challenge, for we are left to carry on the actions and attitudes of Jesus in our world.

EUCHARIST

Historical Development

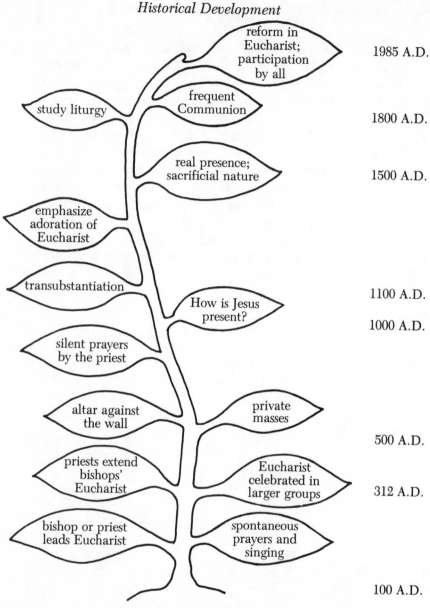

reform in Eucharist; participation by all — 1985 A.D.

frequent Communion — 1800 A.D.

study liturgy

real presence; sacrificial nature — 1500 A.D.

emphasize adoration of Eucharist

transubstantiation — 1100 A.D.

How is Jesus present? — 1000 A.D.

silent prayers by the priest

altar against the wall

private masses — 500 A.D.

priests extend bishops' Eucharist

Eucharist celebrated in larger groups — 312 A.D.

bishop or priest leads Eucharist

spontaneous prayers and singing

100 A.D.

Scriptural Roots

Luke 22:14-20 In remembrance of Jesus
Mark 14:12-14, 22-24 Sacrifice and commitment
Mark 10:38 Can you drink the cup?
Mark 14:25 Eternal dimension
Acts 2:42-47 Central to community
Luke 24:13-35 Recognize Jesus

Luke 9:10-17 Take, bless, break, give
John 6:25-58 Bread of Life
1 Cor 10:16-17 Unity in Christ
1 Cor 11:20-22 Meal with Eucharist
1 Cor 11:23-26 Earliest teaching on Eucharist
1 Cor 11:27-29 Real presence of Christ

THREE

Sacrificing for the Meal— The Eucharist

Then taking bread and giving thanks, he broke it and gave it to them, saying: "This is my body to be given for you. Do this as a remembrance of me." He did the same with the cup after eating, saying as he did so: "This cup is the new covenant in my blood, which will be shed for you."

(Luke 22:19-20)

Scriptural Roots

What happened at table on that night before Jesus died was more than the apostles could comprehend. It would remain a memory that they would never forget. It would become an action central to their lives. It would remain a mystery for all time — the mystery of Jesus' presence in the sharing of bread and wine, the sacrament of the Eucharist.

It might be helpful to realize that references to Eucharist or the "breaking of bread" in scripture mean to include the whole event of gathering in memory of Jesus, recalling his words, and sharing bread and wine blessed in his name. In early times people would not have thought of just the bread and wine as being the Eucharist, but rather, for them, the whole event was part of the sacrament of the Eucharist. The word "eucharist" itself means "thanksgiving." The early community gave thanks again and again for all that Jesus had done for them through his life, death and resurrection.

To begin to understand this sacrament we might try to recall the memories of that sacred evening and feel the commitment the apostles were making.

The words of Jesus that evening, together with his actions, are the first roots of what we call the sacrament of the Eucharist. After breaking the bread he said, "This is my body to be given *for you.*" He loved his disciples so much that he wanted to stay with them, and so he left his sacred memory in the gift of bread broken and wine shared. This gesture summarized the sacrificial dimension of his whole life — the compassion, the risking, the reaching out, the total caring that he exemplified. He had lived for them, now he would die for them and for us that we might live and die for one another. He had shown the power of self-sacrifice throughout his life, and how he left an action in which his people could recall the greatest sacrifice of all, the gift of his life for the redemption of the world.

Jesus went on to say, "Do this in memory of me." He expressed his desire to have them remember his gift of love, the gift of himself. He commissioned them to keep on remembering his act of love. In this way his gift was for all of us. He made it clear that his sacrificial action was to be remembered for the benefit of all who would believe in him. In his absence after the resurrection, the early community came to truly appreciate this gift of his presence. The breaking of bread and the sharing of the cup in his memory became life-sustaining actions for them.

This final meal was more than just a memory, however. It was a commitment, and the twelve apostles could hardly have missed the significance of the gestures that evening. It was the feast of the Passover, the Jewish celebration of their freedom from Egypt. As the meal began, the apostles were thinking of the lamb that was sacrificed as part of that celebration of freedom (Mk 14:12). Jesus was aware that he would be the "lamb" sacrificed for their freedom from sin. Gradually the disciples would realize that they were the lambs who must offer themselves to the Lord, who must die to their own wants if the eucharistic meal was to continue. Eucharist at its roots is a sacrificial meal and all who share in it are challenged to offer themselves for the benefit of others. Without sacrifice, there could be no Eucharist.

As the evening drew on, Jesus' sadness became evident and in simple yet profound words he gave this Passover meal a whole new meaning. "This is my body...this is my blood to be poured out on behalf of many" (Mk 14:22,24). The apostles must have felt the sacrificial commitment that Jesus was making to them, and to the "many." The Lamb of God was choosing to accept death for the freedom of all who accepted his love. He was ready to be broken and poured out to set the world free from the domination of sin and evil.

As the cup of wine was passed around the table that evening, the apostles could hardly help but experience the precious gift of Jesus' love for them. Along with that gift, they must have also felt the commitment they were making as they raised the cup to their lips. Only weeks or months earlier as Jesus approached his passion he had asked them, "Can you drink the cup I shall drink, or be baptized in the same bath of pain as I?" (Mk 10:38). At this final meal Jesus now "took a cup, gave thanks, and passed it to them, and they all drank from it" (Mk 14:23). They *all* drank from it. The apostles were proclaiming in that first Eucharist that they were ready to remain with Jesus no matter what happened. They were putting their lives on the line by putting their hands on the cup. In a very real sense they were responding to Jesus' gift of himself by saying, "Thank you, Jesus, and this is *my* body for you to help bring salvation to all people." Herein lies the essence of the sacrament of the Eucharist. It is a celebration of thanksgiving for Jesus' sacrifice of himself, and it is a celebration of a commitment on the part of all who participate to sacrifice themselves in return for Christ and his people. Without a willingness to give, there is nothing to share. As Catholics, as Christians, it is essential that we attempt to appreciate this original meaning of Eucharist.

In addition to being a meal of remembrance and commitment, the Eucharist also proclaims a future vision, a time when Jesus would be with his followers forever. While Jesus shared his last supper with his apostles on earth, he announced another meal in the reign of God. He said, "I solemnly assure you, I will never again drink of the fruit of the vine until the day when I drink it new in the reign of God" (Mk 14:25). Each time the church celebrates the Eucharist, it proclaims not only its commitment to Christ now, but also its hope of what will one day be in final union with him. That is why the celebration of the Eucharist as part of a funeral is so powerful. I have experienced that power on many occasions. Eucharist proclaims to all who mourn the hope of a final coming together at the table of the Lord. It always contains this eternal dimension, the promise of a never-ending unity with God.

It is no wonder, then, that this sacred action of breaking bread and sharing wine in memory of Jesus took on such a profound significance for the early church. We read in the Acts of the Apostles that the early community "devoted themselves to the apostles' instruction and the communal life, to the breaking of bread and the prayers" (Acts 2:42). The celebration of Eucharist or the "breaking of bread" was a central part of the early community's spiritual growth. When St. Paul wrote to the community at Corinth, he indicated that the teaching about the first Eucharist was essential, and so he carefully "hands it down" to them exactly the way he received it (1 Cor 11:23). It was crucial for their life that they understood the power and significance of this meal.

Perhaps the most beautiful image of the significance

of Eucharist in the early church was captured in the story of the two disciples returning home to Emmaus after the resurrection (Lk 24:13-35). It is a story of the church's struggle to see Jesus and to understand all that he had done in their midst. It tells us that in the breaking of bread "their eyes were opened" to his risen presence, and through that encounter with him, they began to understand the meaning behind his life, death and resurrection. For the apostles who had committed themselves to Jesus the night before he died, and then ran away in the garden, it must have been a very healing and reconciling experience to know that Jesus was ready to break bread with them again. It tells us that, for all who invite Jesus to "stay with them," there is the setting for Eucharist.

It seems clear from the gospels that as the church continued to reflect upon the words and actions of Jesus, it recognized in his earlier ministry some "eucharistic" events. Not only, for example, does each gospel writer include the story of the multiplication of loaves (Mk 6:34-44; Mt 14:13-21; Lk 9:10-17; Jn 6:1-13), but Mark and Luke describe Jesus' actions during that event with the exact same four verbs that they use to recount the last supper. "Then *taking* the five loaves...Jesus raised his eyes to heaven, *pronounced a blessing, broke* the loaves, and *gave* them to the disciples..." (Compare Mk 6:41 and Lk 9:16 with Mk 14:22 and Lk 22:19). It seems that in hindsight they realized what Jesus had been trying to say when he multiplied the loaves. They came to see in this gesture Jesus' desire to be the bread of eternal life for them. The conclusion of that story indicates that the early community felt its responsibility to carry Jesus' nourishing presence to others. Each of the apostles was left with a basket of fragments to distribute. St. John, in telling this story, emphasizes its connection with the Eucharist by using the early church word for eucharistic bread when he describes those fragments (Jn 6:12-13). Eucharist was meant to be multiplied by those who risked sharing themselves.

St. John, in reflecting on the multiplication of loaves, recalls Jesus' words, and how he was ready to be consumed for the life of the world.

"I myself am the living bread
come down from heaven.
If anyone eats this bread
he shall live forever;
the bread I will give
is my flesh for the life of the world" (Jn 6:51).

It is no wonder that the celebration of the Eucharist, especially in times of persecution, became so central to the life of the church. It was a celebration of their unity with their Lord. It was a reaffirmation that with his life in them they would not die. It was an encounter that empowered them to face life and death with the vision of the risen Lord in their eyes.

Eucharist is not only a celebration of unity with the Lord, but also a recognition of unity with all who gather around the table of the Lord. St. Paul expresses this in his letter to the Corinthians where he writes,"Is not the cup of blessing we bless a sharing in the blood of Christ? And is not the bread we break a sharing in the body of Christ? Because the loaf of bread is one, we, many though we are, are one body, for we all partake of the one loaf" (1 Cor 10:16-17).

The sacrament of the Eucharist challenges us to be in unity with each other. Even if there are differences, the breaking of the one loaf calls us to seek unity, and if necessary, to forgive. If there is going to be real sharing, there must be an openness at least to set aside divisive ideas and actions, and to celebrate a common commitment to the Lord. It takes sacrifices to build unity. The sacrament of the Eucharist celebrates the victory of such sacrifices. The Corinthian community had its own divisions (1 Cor 11:18) and Paul's words to them indicate his hope that the remembrance of Jesus' sacrifice could bring healing and renewed unity. The church would wrestle with this aspect of Eucharist throughout history. The eucharistic table was divided through the years and only recently has the hope of unity in the Eucharist been reawakened.

The first letter of Paul to the Corinthians also indicates that in the early days the community had a whole meal as part of their celebration of the Eucharist. It makes us aware that the Christians of those days had their faults too. Paul writes, "When you assemble it is not to eat the Lord's Supper, for everyone is in haste to eat his own supper. One person goes hungry while another gets drunk" (1 Cor 11:20-21). It is perhaps because of abuses such as these that the church began limiting the sacrament of the Eucharist to the sharing of bread and wine only. Those elements captured the memories of Jesus' gift of himself and the sharing of them made his presence real to all who participated.

Paul's words in the following verses (1 Cor 11:23-29) describe the core teaching of the church on the Eucharist. He not only passes on the memory of the last supper exactly the way he received it, but he points out that, "Every time you eat this bread and drink this cup, you proclaim the death of the Lord until he comes" (1 Cor 11:26)! The church could proclaim his death because it represented the victory of salvation. That is why it was celebrated on the first day of the week, the anniversary of the resurrection, which for the early church began Saturday evening after sundown. In celebrating the Eucharist, the people were proclaiming eternal life and their readiness to die with Christ to achieve that life. That proclamation made in unity with one another was their strength, especially in times of persecution. That was the mystery of Jesus' presence among them.

The words of Paul go on to describe the early church's belief regarding the presence of Jesus in the sacrament of the Eucharist. He expresses the importance of recognizing that the bread and wine become the body and blood of the Lord. We read:

> This means that whoever eats the bread or
> drinks of the cup of the Lord unworthily sins
> against the body and blood of the Lord. A man
> should examine himself first; only then should
> he eat of the bread and drink of the cup. He
> who eats and drinks without recognizing the
> body eats and drinks a judgment on himself (1
> Cor 11:27-29).

These words form the basis of the Catholic church's teaching about the *real presence* of Christ in this sacrament. The church from earliest times has always taught that the bread blessed and broken in Jesus' memory becomes his body and the wine becomes his blood. No scripture explains exactly how this happens, but *that* it happens is very clear. Again we face the mystery of how Jesus remains present in these sacred elements.

We do not fully understand the mystery of Christ's presence in Eucharist, but we are convinced that he is truly there. We feel his personal love more powerfully in this sacrament than in any other. Many people have experienced him bring healing to body and heart after receiving his body and blood. His presence in this sacrament brings new peace and wholeness to many who come in expectant faith. It is no wonder that the Eucharist has remained the primary sacrament of the church for all of history.

With this in mind, it is understandable why Paul challenged his people to examine themselves before receiving the Eucharist. It is a profound commitment to say "yes" to the body and blood of Christ. In our day when people ask, "Do I have to go to Mass?" We need to respond, "Are you ready to make the commitment that the Mass demands?" That question is not so much focused on what a person did in the past, but rather, what that person is ready to do in the future. Any sin of the past can be forgiven. The Eucharist is a commitment to invest ourselves in the ongoing work of building the kingdom of God. It is openness to that commitment that makes us ready to sit at table with the Lord.

The sacrament of the Eucharist as we find it in scripture then, is a profound gesture of love expressed in sacrifice—Jesus giving himself to his disciples and the disciples giving themselves to him and to each other. It is a celebration of the victory of life over death, forgiveness over sin, and unity over division — a victory that is won by those who dare to say with Jesus, "This is my body, this is my blood *for you*." It is a commitment to die for the victory of love, to remain faithful to the Victor. It involves an examination of what has been, and an openness to what can be in Jesus. It is a proclamation of the hope of what will one day be when all celebrate at the eternal banquet table of the Lord.

As the Christian community faced the challenges and influences of history, the celebration of the Eucharist took on new shapes and meaning. It is important that we keep in mind its original essence and its original power as we journey through the historical development of this sacrament.

Historical Development

The early church had to develop a way of celebrating the Eucharist in all the various communities that were being formed. The first three centuries of Christian history indicate that the leader of each community also led the main celebration of the Eucharist, and usually did so in the home of a community member. At first the leader of a community may have been a traveling apostle or a prophet or teacher, but later bishops or priests became the community leaders and main celebrants of the Eucharist. These celebrations took place at first on Saturday evening after sundown as part of the Saturday evening meal. As Eucharist became a celebration separate from the whole meal, it began to be celebrated most often on Sunday morning. It was assumed that all members of the community would join in the celebration. They needed to experi-

ence the support and encouragement of each other and
the power of Jesus' presence, especially in times of persecution.

The main framework of these early Eucharists included readings from scripture, prayers for needs, an offering of gifts, a "eucharistic" prayer, and the sharing of
communion. The main celebrant of the Eucharist phrased
the prayers himself and invited all to pray along. These
early liturgies were filled with spontaneous prayers and
singing by the people. It is a beautiful experience when
this happens today. During some liturgies, the people feel
such a strong desire to be part of the celebration that they
spontaneously join in the prayers or begin praying and
worshiping on their own. This is a powerful expression of
our common gratitude to our God and a sign of our common commitment to him.

It is interesting to note that in early times it was common for people to take communion home from the eucharistic liturgy for those who were sick. This practice indicates their belief that Christ was truly present in the bread
and wine, and that his presence in these elements had the
power to bring healing. Since the Second Vatican Council
this practice has been restored. Shut-ins can now share in
what is happening in the community when someone
brings them communion every Sunday.

After 312 A.D. when Christianity became the official
religion of the Roman Empire, the size of the communities increased rapidly and the celebration of the Eucharist
took on a more official character. The bishop presided
over these liturgies and was surrounded by the priests.
More ceremonies and rituals were added to these eucharistic celebrations, which more and more came to resemble
official Roman ceremonies. Even though by this time the
bishop prayed the eucharistic prayer alone, the community was thought of as "concelebrating" with him by their
participation in the singing and other prayers. As the celebration of the Eucharist became enlarged and more offi-

cial, it lost some of the intimacy experienced in this sacrament in earlier times.

While the Eucharist lost some intimacy, it held onto a sense of unity. The early community would build only one church or basilica in the city with only one altar where all gathered at one liturgy on each Sunday. When more than one church became a necessity, they built parish churches as extensions of the bishop's central church. When the Eucharist was celebrated by the priests in these churches, it was done so as a conscious extension of the bishop's liturgy. To dramatize the central importance of being one with the bishop, a piece of the bread from the bishop's Eucharist was sent to each of these extension parishes and dropped into the chalice there as a symbol of unity. This practice indicates the churches' strong sense of commitment to one another and their desire to share at the same eucharistic table.

It was also around this time (384 A.D.) that the liturgy was translated from Greek into Latin and began to be referred to as the Mass. This translation allowed the people to understand more fully what was being proclaimed for while Greek was the common language of earlier centuries, Latin had taken its place as the "people's language." Eucharist was, from earliest times, meant to be a celebration which everyone participated in and understood. The celebration of Mass, however, became locked into the Latin language for many centuries, but in the 1960s through the decision of Vatican II it was restored to the language of the people.

This sense of all the people participating in the celebration of the Lord's Supper began to be lost in the sixth century when priests started saying Masses by themselves. Their original intention was to pray for special needs, but this practice detracted greatly from the original purpose of the Eucharist. By the seventh century these private Masses were so common that churches started having more than one altar, and the altars were placed up against

the wall in order that others might "not be disturbed" by
the celebration of the Mass. What began as a table of
unity for breaking bread and sharing wine together was
now an altar for the priest's private prayers.

As the sacrament of the Eucharist was renewed in the
1960s, the altar was restored to its original central place in
church where the whole community could gather around
and participate together in prayer. I find that once people
have the chance to come forward and gather around the
altar in church, or participate in a more intimate eucharistic sharing, they want to do it more often.

During the Dark Ages (eighth through eleventh centuries) the private character of the Mass began influencing
community Eucharists. We see in the old missals the Mass
prayers change from the use of "we" to "I," and gradually
almost all the prayers were said silently by the priest
alone. By the end of this period of history, the Mass was
no longer celebrated consciously as an action of the community, but had become the personal function of the
priest. The architecture of the churches reflected this understanding by setting the action of the priest farther and
farther from the people. Since the people in the community were no longer actively participating in the eucharistic celebration, their main action became worshiping the
sacred objects of the Mass. They watched and adored the
body and blood of Christ, while the priest performed his
private ceremony. It is hard to tell exactly what brought
this all about, but it certainly did not resemble the intimate communal sharing of that first Eucharist. We see
how the people understood less and less of what was going
on as the priest performed the ritual.

Besides this separation of the action from the people,
a eucharistic piety also developed during the ninth century which accented the unworthiness of the people to receive the body and blood of Christ. This led to the practice of confessing sins before each Mass and less frequent
reception of communion. Communion began to be re-

ceived on the tongue while kneeling. Drinking from the
cup was eliminated altogether. Jesus' original expressions
of love and unity with his people were becoming objects
of fear. While people of this time recognized the sacredness of Christ's presence in the Eucharist, they were losing
the original intention for which he had left this sacred
action. Jesus' desire to remain with his followers through
bread that is broken and a cup that is shared by all was
being overshadowed by the influences of the culture and
the times. The bread and wine once shared as a symbol of
unity, sacrifice and commitment gradually became objects
too "sacred" for the community to receive. With these developments the sacrament of the Eucharist lost much of its
original meaning.

We can also see in these developments the origins the
Benediction and processions with the sacred bread. The
main action of the people had become adoration rather
than communal sharing. There is nothing wrong with
these forms of prayer; however, they are not what the celebration of the Eucharist was at its origin.

It is no wonder, then, that when the theologians of
the 11th and 12th centuries tried to define how Jesus was
present in the Eucharist, they were hard pressed to come
up with a statement. The objects of the Mass had become
separated from their original context of the sacrificial
meal, and no theological language could adequately describe where and how Jesus was present. The church, as
we saw in scripture, had always believed that the bread
and wine became the body and blood of Christ, but that
was easier to understand in the context of a community
celebration where people experienced Jesus' love for them
and could express their commitment to him in return. His
presence was felt in the total encounter. Separated from
this setting, it was hard to describe the mystery of Jesus'
presence in the Eucharist at this point in history. Despite
all this, people still experienced him as they attended
Mass. Jesus' promise to remain with his people remained

in spite of outside influences and human errors. The theologians eventually used the word "transubstantiation" to describe how the substance of the bread and wine is transformed into the body and blood of Christ through the consecrating words of the priest.

The sacrament of the Eucharist remained a private action of the priest from this period on into the sixteenth century. By that time not even the priest would receive communion during the Mass. More and more the bread and wine became objects of worship, totally separated from the context of the first eucharistic meal.

During the 16th century a number of reformers, including Martin Luther, tried to correct the practices surrounding the Mass. Their attempts only led to divisions and disagreements about how Jesus was present in the Eucharist and about the sacrificial nature of that sacrament. Most reformers taught that Jesus was only symbolically present in the bread and wine. Luther taught that Christ was truly present in the bread and wine, but only at the moment of the consecration when the passion was commemorated, and at communion when the death of the Lord was proclaimed. The Catholic church, at the Council of Trent in 1563, restated its belief that the bread and wine, through the consecrating words of the priest, *become* and *remain* the body and blood of Christ. These diverse teachings have remained to the present. The sacrament of unity and common commitment had become a source of controversy and division.

These differences regarding how Jesus was present in the Eucharist were widened by disagreements as to whether the sacrifice of the Mass reenacted Jesus' sacrifice on the cross, or just commemorated that sacrifice. Again, the fact that the celebration of the Eucharist at this time did not resemble the sacrificial meal of the first Eucharist made this debate hard to solve. The Catholic church continued to teach that Christ's sacrifice on the cross was renewed and commemorated in each Mass. Recently this understanding has found agreement among other Christian denominations.

The main question, regarding this issue is not, how is Jesus' sacrifice on the cross commemorated in the Eucharist, but rather, what sacrifice is each of us ready to make to bring Jesus' risen presence to the community with whom we are celebrating? We are grateful that Jesus gave his body and blood for us. The challenge of the sacrament of the Eucharist is to say in return, "Lord, this is my body, this is my blood for you." In this way we make the sacrifice of Jesus present and visible to the people in our lives. That is what the apostles were asked to do as they shared the bread and drank from the cup. This is the more important sacrificial dimension of the Eucharist.

The sacrament of the Eucharist in the Catholic church remained, until the present century, an action to be watched by the people. Beginning in the 19th century and continuing in the 20th, theologians were studying the sources of the Catholic tradition regarding this sacrament. In 1905 Pope Pius X encouraged more frequent sharing in communion, emphasizing the importance of people participating in the celebration. Further study of this sacrament in the 1940s and 50s set the stage for the further renewal of the Second Vatican Council.

With Vatican II (1962-65) the Catholic church continued to try to restore the celebration of the Eucharist to its original meaning and form. This included changes such as celebrating the liturgy in the language of the people, moving the altar to a more central place, giving more emphasis to the reading of scripture, encouraging more frequent reception of communion, eliminating the many unnecessary signs and gestures that accumulated during the Middle Ages, and restoring the action of drinking from the cup. These and other changes have brought our present-day celebration of the Eucharist closer to its scriptural meaning, making it more like the sacred celebration that Jesus left during that last evening with his disciples.

These changes have helped us on the road to Christian unity as well. Though there are still specific guidelines for sharing the Eucharist with other Christians, the Catholic church is taking steps toward one eucharistic table. As all Christian churches go back to the scriptural roots of this sacrament, the hope of a common eucharistic sharing begins to dawn.

Through the 1960s and 70s the structure of the Mass was revised to make it more of a community celebration. We now have the framework to make the Eucharist happen, to experience Christ in one another, to feel the commitment we make when we say "Amen" to the body and blood of Christ. Christ is really present in the bread and wine, but we are discovering as well the powerful presence of Jesus among the people who gather together, committed to one another's health and growth. People are growing in a greater awareness of Jesus' presence in his word read at the Eucharist, and an appreciation of his presence experienced both in communal songs and in the silent moments of prayer. In healing Masses in some parishes, people are discovering the healing and reconciling power of breaking bread and sharing the cup in memory of Jesus' great love. During these liturgies there is a conscious focusing on Jesus' healing presence in the scripture readings, in his body and blood, in the community gathered, and in the sacrament of anointing which follows the Mass. People go away from these celebrations speaking of how they have felt the Lord's healing and transforming love. It seems only appropriate that as we receive and encounter the same Jesus who healed and forgave long ago, we should experience healing and forgiveness within ourselves.

As we grew in discovering the power of committing ourselves to Jesus and to one another in the Eucharist, we will see even greater things happen. What Jesus did for his apostles on the evening of that first Eucharist was to celebrate the inner freedom he had in doing the Father's will.

He showed them that it was in the giving of themselves that they would know real inner freedom and peace. People have felt that freedom and peace through this sacrament, and they have experienced healing as they celebrate this meal in memory of him. They have come to know his deep love for them as they remember this gift of himself.

The apostles did not fully understand the mystery of how Jesus would remain present to them. We may never understand it either. It is our challenge as Christians to discover all that we can about Jesus' gift of himself in the Eucharist in order that we might enrich our lives and bring others to experience that gift. We can learn from the errors of history, and then participate in making the celebration of the Eucharist a true encounter with the risen Lord.

RECONCILIATION

Historical Development

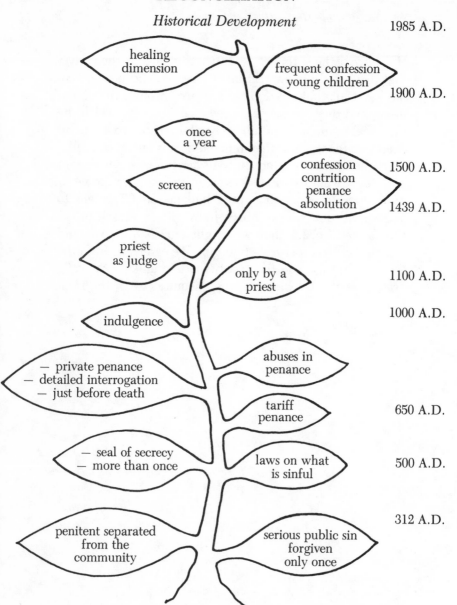

1985 A.D.

healing dimension

frequent confession young children

1900 A.D.

once a year

confession contrition penance absolution

1500 A.D.

1439 A.D.

screen

priest as judge

only by a priest

1100 A.D.

1000 A.D.

indulgence

— private penance
— detailed interrogation
— just before death

abuses in penance

tariff penance

650 A.D.

— seal of secrecy
— more than once

laws on what is sinful

500 A.D.

312 A.D.

penitent separated from the community

serious public sin forgiven only once

Scriptural Roots

John 20:19-21 Jesus' gift of peace
John 3:17,19 Not to condemn
Luke 7:36-50 Penitent woman
John 4:4-42 Woman at the well
Luke 19:1-10 Zacchaeus
Luke 23:34 Father, forgive them
John 5:1-15 Unwilling to reconcile

Matthew 18:18 Binding and loosing
1 Corinthians 5:1-5 Sinner cast out
2 Corinthians 2:5-8 Sinner forgiven
Luke 15:11-32 Divine mercy
2 Corinthians 2:11 Power of evil
John 8:9-11 Adulterous woman
James 5:16 Forgiveness and healing

FOUR

Laying Sins to Rest— Reconciliation

On the evening of that first day of the week, even though the disciples had locked the doors of the place where they were for fear of the Jews, Jesus came and stood before them, "Peace be with you," he said. When he had said this he showed them his hands and his side. At the sight of the Lord the disciples rejoiced. "Peace be with you," he said again.

> "As the Father has sent me,
> so I send you."
>
> (John 20:19-21)

Scriptural Roots

"Peace be with you," Jesus said, and the disciples knew that he still loved them; he was still with them. To those who may well have been feeling guilty for running away, afraid of what Jesus would say, and unworthy of ever being in his presence again, Jesus gives his *peace*, his gift of reconciliation. The disciples had seen Jesus forgive others, but on this occasion they experienced the power of his mercy themselves. With his gift of peace, their hearts were set free of guilt, fear and alienation, free to live again in his Spirit.

With this gift came the mandate to forgive others, to offer the opportunity for others to be set free by the generous mercy of the risen Lord. Here is the birth of the sacrament of reconciliation, a sacrament of inner peace.

The sacrament of reconciliation took on many and varied forms throughout history, but essentially it is a sacrament of inner peace flowing from Jesus' extravagant mercy and love. Jesus accepted death on the cross as his ultimate act of love to give all people the chance to be set free from the bondage of sin. The sacrament of reconciliation would remain the opportunity to encounter the Lord's mercy in times of guilt, his peace in times of fear, and his acceptance in times of alienation. To all who sinned, it would be the chance to experience reconciliation, the privilege to encounter the Reconciler himself.

Jesus' whole being exemplified a desire to bring ultimate peace to people. A significant part of his mission of peace was his ministry of reconciliation. The reason he came into the world was to offer salvation, to offer life to people bound in sin and darkness. St. John writes, "God did not send the Son into the world to condemn the world, but that the world might be saved through him" (Jn 3:17). Jesus came to rescue us from sin, not to condemn us for our failures. He came as a source of life. He came as a light to guide us when we had lost our way in darkness. If anyone was to experience condemnation in his presence, it was because they chose to turn away from the light. John writes,

> "The judgment of condemnation is this:
> the light came into the world,
> but men loved darkness rather than light
> because their deeds were wicked" (Jn 3:19).

Jesus' goodness, his love, his personality made sin obvious, but to all who came to him in sorrow, he offered reconciliation. We see this in his encounter with Simon and the penitent woman (Lk 7:36-50). Simon thinks that Jesus does not know "who and what sort of woman" was touching him, but Jesus makes it clear that he is well aware of her sinful past. He goes on to point out the depth of her sorrow for her sins and all the gestures of love that she used to express her desire for reconciliation. Jesus' concluding words offer her the gift that only he can give. "Go now in peace" (Lk 7:50). Simon is left wishing that he had the courage and humility to repent and be at peace with his guest.

Jesus was not afraid to eat with sinners and to talk with them. He had a way of loving the goodness in them and his expression of that love was their invitation to repent. To all who accepted that invitation he offered abundant mercy and lasting peace.

The disciples and the church were left with the mission of continuing the ministry of reconciliation that was so central to the life of Jesus. It was obvious that this ministry was not tied to any particular ritual or gesture, but simply flowed from the personality of the Reconciler himself. His unconditional love, his unbelievable gentleness, his simple goodness challenged people to examine themselves and deal with their sins. The disciples themselves had experienced his gentle love and saw the power it had to bring people to repentance and inner peace. They knew the ministry of reconciliation would begin with radiating that gentle, accepting love of Jesus. It is that love which forms the basis of the sacrament of reconciliation.

We can begin to understand this sacrament by walking with Jesus along the roads of Palestine and watching him personally invite hurting and guilty people to the freedom of reconciliation. As we observe Jesus minister to the thirsty woman at the well (Jn 4:4-42), for example, we see his persistent, gentle love melt her defenses and bring about forgiveness and real peace. When she is ready to face her past sins, Jesus helps her name the real issue of pain and bondage in her life. He says to her, "Go call your husband, and then come back here." He knows that she must choose to change before she can be free, and his unconditional love gives her the space to make that choice.

"I have no husband," was her reply, but Jesus' desire to set her free from the burden of sin is so strong that her lying response does not bring condemnation; rather, it brings an expression of persistent concern.

"You are right in saying you have no husband!" Jesus says, and then he goes on to point out the real reason for her inner fear and thirst. "The fact is, you have had five, and the man you are living with now is not your husband. What you said is true." Jesus' expression of understanding and acceptance gives this woman the space to repent and experience true inner peace.

Often as priests in ministering the sacrament of reconciliation we meet people like this woman who are thirsting to be set free, but struggle to name the real issue that binds them. We are challenged to pray for the ability to radiate the persistent, gentle love of Jesus so that eventually people have the courage to name what it is that is causing discord in their lives. Once it is admitted, the words of Jesus' forgiveness and acceptance can bring inner freedom and peace. Those who experience the freeing forgiveness of the Lord often tell others of the peace that flows from letting go of sin.

Jesus' desire to forgive was evident in that he went out of his way to enter into the homes of sinners in order to bring them real peace. He saw good in people when they were not able to see good in themselves, and his loving acceptance gave them space to come out of their bondage of sin. We see this as we watch Jesus minister to Zacchaeus (Lk 19:1-10). Jesus' words of affirmation, "Zacchaeus, hurry down, I mean to stay at your house today," draw this man out of his tree and give him the security to be reconciled, even to make up for his sins. Jesus' desire and readiness to enter into this sinner's home and offer the peace of forgiveness brought about a true experience of reconciliation evidenced by his willingness to change. He tells Jesus, "I give half my belongings, Lord, to the poor. If I have defrauded anyone in the least, I pay him back fourfold."

Jesus makes it clear at the conclusion of this story that he came into the world to "search out and save" those who were lost and in this incident he shows us one way to accomplish that. He does not tell Zacchaeus what he did wrong, but gives him the space to change by affirming the good he saw in him. He does not judge him for his sinful actions, but enters into Zacchaeus' life in a way that he could *feel* accepted and invites him to the peace of reconciliation. This gesture of Jesus to eat with sinners shows his desire to bring out the good in people and to help them let go of sin.

The story of Zacchaeus indicates to us the need for a minister of reconciliation, and indeed the whole Christian community, to reach out in love and acceptance to those bound in fear and sin. It challenges us to affirm the good in people in such a positive way that they feel the acceptance and the freedom to let go of the bondage of sin. We are called to enter their "homes" not to condone sin, but to offer reconciliation. In this way we see how the effectiveness of the sacrament of reconciliation depends to a large extent on the Christian community exemplifying the intense love of Jesus and helping people respond to that love with a decision to repent.

Once people are drawn to repentance and sorrow for their sins, the sacrament of reconciliation is the opportunity to experience the Lord's personal acceptance, to lay down the burden of sin, and to hear the Lord's loving words of forgiveness. It is the final celebration of peace with those who have been drawn out of alienation by the love made visible by one or several community members. In this sense, each of us is called to be a minister of reconciliation.

Jesus' ministry of reconciliation not only involved going out of his way to reach out to sinners, but it also meant forgiving those who had done harm to him. His words from the cross, "Father, forgive them; they do not know what they are doing" (Lk 23:34), demonstrated his ultimate love and acceptance of people. These words left his followers the greatest challenge of forgiveness. They were called to minister the mercy of Jesus even when the pain caused by sin was still felt. The ministry of reconciliation challenges the Christian to move beyond the human

desire to retaliate and offer the peace of divine forgiveness. In the sacrament of reconciliation this is the challenge of the priest, a challenge that can be met only
through a close relationship with the Master of Peace.

While our journey with Jesus through the scriptures
makes us aware of our call to minister mercy and forgiveness, it also shows us that ultimate reconciliation depends
upon the people's decision to repent and be sorry for their
sins. Jesus' initial action to set people free of sin only
brought about reconciliation when they responded with a
decision to change. Zacchaeus expressed his decision to
change by offering his money to the poor and to those he
had cheated. The man lying by the sheep pool whom Jesus cured physically was not ready to change his heart and
so Jesus' invitation to reconciliation was rendered ineffec-
tive. Jesus had cured him and then invited him to be truly
at peace with the words, "Remember, now, you have been
cured. Give up your sins so that something worse may not
overtake you." The man ignored Jesus' invitation to inner
freedom and went instead to report Jesus to the Jews (Jn
5:1-15). Jesus' desire to bring about reconciliation was sti-
fled by the man's unwillingness to attempt a change in his
life. Jesus did not condemn him, but he could not force
him to change either.

Perhaps that is why when Jesus taught his disciples
about the ministry of forgiving, he made them aware that
they could not force reconciliation (Mt 18:15-17). They
were called upon to radiate the love of Jesus, so that in the
face of that love, people could recognize their faults and
repent. If they ignored the community's invitation to reconciliation, the church was to treat them as outsiders. If
the community's witness and words could not bring a person to repentance and a change of heart, Jesus' mercy
could not enter into their being and loosen the bondage of
sin. Jesus expressed this when he said, "Whatever you declare bound on earth shall be held bound in heaven, and
whatever you declare loosed on earth shall be loosed in

heaven" (Mt 18:18). Jesus respects the freedom of a person to remain in bondage.

This "binding" or casting out of the unrepented sinner was not to be seen as a sign of not caring. In fact, it is exactly the opposite. St. Paul points this out when he challenges the community at Corinth to cast out the man in their midst who is committing a serious public sin by "living with his father's wife" (1 Cor 5:1-5). Paul explains that he should be bound from being in the community so that he comes to his senses and saves his soul. The binding is only temporary to bring a sinner to repentance and ultimate reconciliation. In this case, it seems that the man changed his ways, for in his second letter to the Corinthians Paul tells the community to welcome him back into their midst (2 Cor 2:5-8).

Drawing people to a decision for reconciliation remained a challenge for the church. Jesus, as we saw, did this at times through his words, but most often by his intense love of people and his affirmation of the good in them. He allowed sinners the freedom to bind themselves in sin, yet when they chose to be sorry, he offered them the peace of his mercy. He taught his disciples to do the same.

The parable of the forgiving father (Lk 15:11-32) expresses in picture form his attitude of compassion and freedom. The father's love in the story, representing the love of God, does not bind or force the sons, but allows them the freedom to accept it or turn away. It is this consistent, free love of the father that makes the younger son "come to his senses" and choose to return home. When people have seriously sinned and then come to their senses in light of the love they once felt, the sacrament of reconciliation is the celebration of their coming home. It is the chance to feel the arms of the Father wrapped around them in love.

If we realize that the young son had committed the worst conceivable sin of his day by asking for his inheritance early, we can see an even deeper message in this parable. Jesus was saying to all who listened that *no sin* is beyond the mercy of God. All Jesus asks is that people "come to their senses" and repent of their failures. Then his mercy can set them free to live as they were created to live.

This parable also points out the power of verbalizing our sins, hearing words of forgiveness, and feeling the embrace of acceptance. The younger son apparently knew he would be forgiven by his father, but he would never have *felt* it without that loving embrace and the words of acceptance. His vision of what the father would say was so much less than the father's extravagant welcome of love. This welcome of love made him feel lovable again.

In this light, the sacrament of reconciliation is truly a gift, a privilege. We may know that the Father forgives us, but it is a special gift to have a place where we can *experience* his acceptance and mercy. Sometimes people ask me, "Why do I have to go to confession? Can't God forgive me on his own?" Their question tells me that they have never experienced the peace of verbally pouring out their heart to the Lord, and then hearing words of forgiveness for their personal sins. God forgives, but as human beings we need to experience that forgiveness in the human gestures of love and acceptance. Many people have never had the privilege of such an experience.

Perhaps that is why many people identify with the older son in the parable. This son knows that he is in good standing with the father, but never *feels* the father's love, never experiences "being at home" with the father. Physically he was in the father's house, but emotionally he felt alienated, alone, and resentful. He, too, needed to come to the father and hear his words of affirmation, to hear him say, "I love you, son. You are a good person. Whatever I have is yours because I love you."

We all alienate ourselves from God and from others at times, and it is a gift to have a place to verbalize our failures, to hear the Lord's words of forgiveness for us, and to feel hands of acceptance embrace us. There is no healthier way to deal with sin, there is no more powerful experience of the Lord's deep love and affirmation.

I have experienced the power of this sacrament myself, and I have watched countless others experience the same. I recall a young man who, after many years of resisting, finally came to the sacrament of reconciliation. Like many Christians, he was a good person, but he carried the weight of unspoken sins. His encounter with the Lord in reconciliation brought him a new, deep, inner peace. A couple of days later, his wife called saying, "I can't believe the change in him since he went to the sacrament. He has really changed. He seems so much more peaceful." Within a couple of weeks her fear of this sacrament was overcome by her desire to experience that same peace. After many years of "just talking to God about it" she experienced God's deep love and acceptance of her in this sacrament. Her testimony of inner peace brought many others to celebrate this sacrament of peace.

Jesus knew that his followers would fail at times and so he commissioned them to minister mercy in his name. He wanted them to feel his peace even after failure, even if their failures were not serious. He did not want them to live in the fear and alienation caused by unforgiven sin. Jesus did not want his followers to be overcome by the power of evil that can enter a person through unresolved areas of sin. St. Paul expressed this value for the ministry of forgiveness when he wrote, "Any forgiving I have done has been for your sakes and, before Christ, to prevent Satan — whose guile we know too well — from outwitting us" (2 Cor 2: 10-11). Paul was aware that unrepented sin was a doorway for a spirit of evil or darkness to enter into a person. He was concerned that the members of the community keep one another safe from the power of the evil one by bringing each other to the mercy of the Lord. We are all called to be ministers of reconciliation in this sense, not by judging others, but by radiating the unconditional love and acceptance of Jesus.

Jesus not only wanted to protect his followers from the power of evil, but he also sought to keep them healthy. He knew that the burden of unrepented sin caused inner turmoil and made a person susceptible to illness. His ministry of reconciliation was part of his ministry of healing. His intense love and affirmation gave sinners the space to let go of their sins and experience inner healing and peace. The New Testament church seems to have recognized this close relationship between reconciliation and healing, for in the letter of James we read, "Declare your sins to one another, and pray for one another, that you may find healing" (Jas 5:16). The sacrament of reconciliation is a beautiful opportunity to experience not only the forgiveness of Jesus, but also his healing. I find that after people have just confessed their sins in the sacrament of reconciliation, they are often very receptive to a prayer of inner healing for the wounded emotions or memories in their lives that may be part of their patterns of sin. Through the prayer of forgiveness and inner healing they experience the peace of Jesus.

The ministry of reconciliation as Jesus did it does not mean that he condoned sin, but that he saw goodness in the sinner's heart. We see this when the crowd brought the woman caught in adultery to him (Jn 8:1-11). Jesus spoke out clearly on the side of faithfulness in marriage. His acceptance and forgiveness of this woman is not an acceptance of her sin, but an affirmation of her desire to begin again on the road to faithfulness. He loves the woman so much that he does not want her to stay trapped in sin. He wants her to have life and ultimate salvation, and so offers her an alternative to the punishment suggested by the Jewish law. What the stones could not bring out in this woman, his love could. He offers her forgiveness and then calls her to change. He gives her a way to true happiness by his final words, "You may go. But from now on, avoid this sin."

The sacrament of reconciliation, in this same way, is not an acceptance of sin, but a recognition of sin and a celebration of a person's desire for forgiveness and conversion. It expresses Jesus' love for the sinner, not his love of sin. It is an encounter of the sinner with the Lord to help that person turn away from sin and begin again to live in peace. This encounter with the forgiving Lord often helps people forgive themselves. I have seen many people grow in acceptance of themselves through hearing the forgiving words of Jesus.

The scriptures clearly show us Jesus' desire and his power to minister inner peace through forgiveness. This desire was so central to his whole life mission that he taught his followers to do the same. He showed them during his lifetime the gentle, accepting love that affirmed the goodness in people and led them to repentance. He promised to remain with them when "binding the sinner" was the only road to ultimate reconciliation and peace. He demonstrated the importance of being present to the sinner, knowing that the times of serious guilt, feeling hands of acceptance and hearing words of forgiveness were necessary to experience real peace. These words and attitudes of Jesus are the roots of the sacrament of reconciliation.

The disciples, indeed all of us, were challenged to continue Jesus' ministry of reconciliation, to exemplify his loving personality, to re-enact his attitudes and words of forgiveness. His message to the disciples on that evening of the resurrection, "Peace be with you," would be a constant reminder of his extravagant mercy and persistent love. The growing church was left to continue ministering this mercy and love with the gentleness of the Master.

Historical Development

The evidence is scanty regarding the ministry of reconciliation in the post-New Testament church. While it seems that the early Christians continued to declare their individual sins to one another, they struggled to minister reconciliation to someone who offended the whole community by a serious public sin. Most written history about the sacrament of reconciliation deals with these serious public situations, yet the fact that Christian communities grew and were admired for their loving witness is evidence that the ministry of reconciliation was happening among the community members during the early centuries.

The early Christians carried on Jesus' attitude of forgiving among themselves, but they found it a great challenge to balance that attitude with their strong emphasis on a person's baptismal commitment. They put so much stress on the commitment made at baptism to live according to Jesus' way, that when someone publicly broke that commitment through serious sin, they questioned whether such a person could ever again live in full union with the community. They agreed that the sacrament of baptism-confirmation forgave all previous sins, but they searched for a way to deal with serious sins committed after a person had become a Christian.

Certain heretical groups in these early centuries such as the Montanists and the Novatianists taught that some serious public sins committed after baptism were unforgivable. They were referring to the sins of apostasy, murder and adultery. In response to these heresies the church recalled that Peter had committed apostasy by denying that he knew Jesus, yet Jesus forgave him. A document dated about A.D. 150 called the *Shepherd of Hermes* indicated that the church always held that any sin was forgivable as long as a person was sorry and sought to be reunited with the Lord.

The early church was very intent on the need for reparation or penance for sins as part of the reconciling process. The stress on the need for severe penances does not seem to stem from the words of Jesus, however, but may have been an influence of the philosophies of that time period. Part of this emphasis flows from the church's stress on the seriousness of the baptismal commitment. Christians in these times took very seriously the words they said when as adults they publicly promised to live in accord with the values and attitudes of Jesus their Lord.

It is important to realize also that the ministry of reconciliation in the early centuries was intimately connected with the need for the community to give an exemplary witness of love to others. The principal way of teaching the love of Jesus to people who did not know him was the good life witness of the community members. If any members publicly broke that witness through sin, they seriously hurt the witness of the whole community. This might help us understand why the early church struggled to determine if and how often they should forgive anyone who committed such a serious public sin after baptism. For reasons not fully known to us, they agreed that such a person could be forgiven only once in their lifetime. We can see why the sacrament of penance would gradually be delayed until the late years of a Christian's life lest this chance for sacramental forgiveness be used up too soon.

The procedure for dealing with Christians who committed a serious public sin was quite detailed and severe. After confessing to the bishop, who represented the whole community, people were enrolled in the order of penitents and were dressed in goat's hair, symbolizing separation from the sheep of Christ. They were also covered with ashes as a symbol of their penitential state. In some ways they were treated as persons seeking to enter the Christian community for the first time. It was as if they had to be readmitted. They would have to leave the celebration of the Eucharist before the prayer of the faithful like those seeking baptism, and they were obliged to fast, to pray, and to give alms to the poor with the guidance of a sponsor. In addition to these things, the penitents were forbidden to do business, have marital relations, or enter military service. After a suitable period of such public penance, they were readmitted to the community during the celebration of the Eucharist on Holy Thursday. On that day they could again share in the meal of unity.

This procedure of reconciliation was not used frequently. This infrequency indicates the tension in the early church between taking the baptismal commitment seriously and desiring to minister Jesus' mercy even after serious sin. That tension was not easy to resolve. Even today it remains a part of the ministry of reconciliation as the church tries to reconcile Christians who publicly live in disharmony with the teachings of Jesus. There may never be an easy solution to this tension.

The small communities of the second and third centuries witnessed to a certain idealism and openness. Members of these communities would publicly admit their less serious sins to the whole community and gladly accept public penance as a means of expressing their sorrow for those sins. Their understanding of penance, though a bit rigorous, was connected to their deep sense of community and their keen awareness of how their sins hurt the whole community. They willingly submitted to the judgment of the community. They gladly accepted penance for sins as a way of expressing their love for each other and for the Lord.

When Christianity became the official religion of the Roman Empire in the early 300s, the communities increased rapidly in size and the individual commitment to the community in general was less intense. The idealism and openness of the earlier centuries waned. People were less likely to admit their sins to everyone in public. As a result, by the end of the fourth century there is a gradual decline in the practice of public penance.

During the fifth and sixth centuries many laws were developed concerning what was sinful and what penance was appropriate for particular sins. Through this period the procedure for dealing with serious public sins came to be called canonical penance and focused primarily on forcing the penitent to make due reparation for sins. Toward the end of this period, the private celebration of penance became the rule and more stress was placed on the confessing of sins. At this time the sacrament came to be called confession and could be received more than once. Less serious sins were submitted and appropriate penances were assigned.

Confessors at this time were not necessarily bishops or priests, but included other people who through their words and personality could express the forgiveness of Jesus and the community. The church has always recognized certain people as being particularly gifted as confessors. Perhaps there will be a time when the church will not need to limit that ministry to priests and bishops.

It is interesting to note that by the end of the sixth century the church developed the idea of the seal of secrecy in confession. This meant that no part of the confession could be repeated to anyone. This is still a part of the sacrament today.

As we have seen, the early church's form of the sacrament of reconciliation in the first centuries dealt almost exclusively with serious public sins and was modeled primarily on Jesus' words about binding and loosing (Mt 18:15-18). After people spent time bound outside the community doing penance, they were freed to enter again into the life of the community. While this was the "official" ministry of reconciliation, we can assume that the mercy and forgiveness of Jesus was shared among Christians as they grew through misunderstandings and personal failures. There is no written record of this type of reconciliation, but the growth of the communities is evidence that it occurred.

During the seventh century a new form of the sacrament of confession was brought to the continent of Europe by the Irish monks who had been influenced by the Celtic communities. This was a more private form of confession or penance that was initially used for priests and religious. It gradually became the method of dealing with sin among the laity.

This new form of the sacrament came to be called tariff penance since the focus was on the priest or monk assigning the appropriate penance to the penitent, which he did only after a private detailed interrogation. This form of penance treated sin as a private affair, almost eliminating any awareness of the communal effects of sin which was so strong in the earlier centuries among Christians. Unlike the earlier forms of penance, the penitents were absolved of their sins and could return to the Eucharist before they completed their penance. This form of penance had the framework to minister the mercy of Jesus in a very personal way. It contained beautiful penitential prayers and it could be repeated over and over.

In practice, however, it seems the church grew farther and farther from Jesus' ministry of reconciliation. By the late seventh century, for example, the focus of this sacrament was on developing penitential books that told the priest what penance was appropriate for each sin and even showed what substitute penance would be of equal worth. From the 7th to 11th centuries, many abuses developed around this sacrament such as the payment of money as a substitute for doing penance, even to the point of confessors demanding money for the forgiveness of sins. For this reason, by the fourteenth century, a screen was placed between the confessor and penitent to protect the penitent from such demands. (Recently, in the renewal of this sacrament, the screen has been removed since its original purpose no longer applies and its elimination allows the priest to minister the forgiveness of Jesus in a more personal and healing way.)

The emphasis on doing penance for sins without an awareness of the effects of sin on the community led to various nonscriptural practices and ideas. At times, instead of doing the penance themselves, people had their serfs do the penance for them. Prayers were said instead of doing an action in reparation for sins, and gradually the concept of indulgences was invented as a way of giving a certain amount of value to these prayers and actions. People developed a sense of trying to appease God for sins rather than feeling loved and cherished by him as a result of his abundant mercy. We also see that because of the strong emphasis on doing extensive penances for sins, people began putting the sacrament of reconciliation off until just before death. That cut down on the length of the penance, but it kept people from experiencing the freeing and healing power of Jesus' mercy during their earlier years. Since the sacrament of the anointing of the sick was always associated with the confessing of sins, this development also caused that sacrament to be put off until just before death, as we shall see in the next chapter.

Perhaps the most devastating ramification of the developments from this period was that the sacrament which was originally intended to re-enact the mercy and forgiveness of Jesus became an occasion for interrogation and judgment. The minister of the sacrament had the role of a judge rather that the one who proclaimed the healing and forgiving love of Jesus. What began as a place of acceptance and recommitment became a place of fear and alienation. We can rejoice that in our time we are making moves to undo these developments and restore this sacrament to its scriptural form and intent.

The period of the 12th to the 14th centuries was a time when various teachings on penance were discussed. During that time the church tried to identify the essential elements of this sacrament. For the previous centuries the need to *do penance* for sins was stressed. At this time some taught that the *confessing* of sins to a priest was essential for forgiveness. (We might note that by this time only a priest could minister the sacrament.) Other theologians held that *contrition* or a contrite heart on the part of the penitent was the most important element in this sacrament of forgiveness, while still others taught that the *absolution* by a priest was essential to the sacrament of penance. This emphasis on the absolution by the priest caused many people to think that the priest forgives sins, whereas in reality he only ministers the mercy of Jesus.

By the Council of Florence in 1439 the church came to define penance as a sacrament consisting of contrition of heart on the part of the penitent, oral confession of one's sins to a priest, doing a penance, and absolution by a priest. These actions celebrated in faith were believed to effect the forgiveness of sins. We see how the church was trying to define in concrete form the mystery of encountering Jesus' extravagant mercy. All those elements may be part of the ministry of reconciliation, but the way they are done can greatly affect whether or not the sinner experiences Jesus' love and mercy.

The reformers of the 16th century had various responses to this teaching on penance. Luther accepted penance as a sacrament but saw absolution not as the power to forgive but as a means of arousing faith in the sinner to receive the mercy of God. For him, faith in God's abundant mercy was more important that the doing of a penance for sins. Calvin reflected a similar understanding, but denied the sacramentality of penance. At the Council of Trent in 1551, the Catholic church reaffirmed its teaching on penance as a sacrament and on the necessity of penance to forgive mortal sins. We see how each of the Christian churches was seeking to capture the essence of Jesus' ministry of reconciliation. For the next 400 years they would stand divided over the mystery of forgiveness flowing from Jesus' act of redemption on the cross.

Throughout this time period until 1905 the sacrament of penance was generally received once a year as was the sacrament of the Eucharist. The pope's encouragement of frequent reception of communion in that year led to the frequent celebration of penance. People began to list the number of their sins and to confess them, sometimes every week. With the recent renewal of the sacrament, people are being encouraged to confess serious sins or to confess patterns of sinfulness that develop in their Christian journey. The less frequent celebration of this sacrament allows people to take the sacrament more seriously and to experience its freeing power in a fuller way.

In 1910 the church put forth a decree stating that children by the age of seven had the *right* to receive the sacrament of penance. Gradually people understood this to mean that children at this age were *obliged* to receive this sacrament before they could receive the Eucharist. The decree never intended to mandate that practice. It seems appropriate in working with young children to begin teaching them the effects of sin at this age and to celebrate with them communal reconciliation or inner peace services in ways they can understand and experience Jesus' love and mercy. I find it more appropriate to lead children into the *individual celebration* of the sacrament of reconciliation as we know it when they reach the age of 11 or 12. I have watched many of the children of our parish truly experience the peace and forgiveness of Jesus through this encounter. They can understand the words of God's mercy found in scripture and appreciate the gift of forgiveness that Jesus offers personally to them. This teaches them a pattern for dealing with sin and experiencing the power of reconciliation for the rest of their lives.

Through the work of the Second Vatican Council (1962-1965) the sacrament of penance was revised in form and renamed the sacrament of reconciliation, indicating its new emphasis of reconciling the sinner to God and the community as in scriptural times. It was taken out of the realm of the dark confessional to a comfortable place where the priest could make the penitent feel welcome and minister Jesus' mercy and affirmation. The reading of God's word was introduced as a way of bathing the penitent in the assurance of God's love.

The new rites of reconciliation include a private celebration and a communal celebration. The private form of reconciliation (Rite I) was retained to deal with serious sin, individual sinful patterns, and the private pastoral needs of the penitent. A new communal form of this sacrament (Rite II) was developed to emphasize the communal effects of sins and forgiveness. It allows for a private expression of sins, but often does not afford as much time to talk privately as Rite I. A totally communal form of reconciliation (Rite III) was developed for cases of extreme emergency when there is no time for individual reconciliation. This rite does not allow time to deal with serious individual sins since all of its parts are communal in nature. Each of these forms is meant to help us as sinful Christians to experience the extravagant mercy and love of Jesus.

The revised sacrament of reconciliation demands more of the minister than it did in some of its older forms. He is called much more than in the past to be a witness of the Lord's gentle mercy and open acceptance. At times the priest himself may be very uncomfortable trying to make the penitent feel comfortable. He may not be at ease with offering a comforting embrace or a consoling hand. I know that at times I and some of my brother priests have not ministered the forgiveness of Jesus as well as it could be done.

History has shown that many errors have been made regarding the sacrament of reconciliation. Recent changes in this sacrament have also caused misunderstandings and hurts. Things were said and done through the recent years of change that caused confusion and alienation. People are now moving beyond those misunderstanding and hurts to discover the freeing and healing power of this precious sacrament.

As a minister of healing and a counselor, I have come to recognize the importance of verbalizing our failures and hearing the Lord's words of forgiveness for our personal sins. The sacrament of reconciliation affords that opportunity. It is truly a privilege. It is a gift to have such an occasion to experience the abundant mercy and forgiveness of the Reconciler himself, and to know that he loves us despite our failures. It is a gift to have someone who cares enough to help us wrestle with sin, to stand against evil, and to assure us that no sin, no matter how serious, can withstand the power of Jesus' love and mercy.

Many of the Christian churches are recognizing the power of having a place to reconcile with the Lord and a person who will minister his mercy and his gentle care. I believe that we will see a revival of this sacrament among all the Christian churches as we lay aside the fears and differences of the past and seek to reenact the gentle, forgiving love of the one who laid down his life for us all. As Christians it is appropriate, and indeed mandatory, that we continue seeking ways to enable people to encounter the Reconciler, and the peace that flows from his mercy.

ANOINTING OF THE SICK

Historical Development

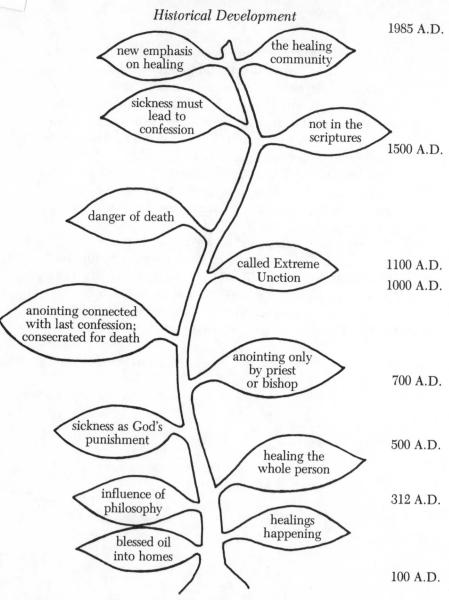

1985 A.D.

new emphasis on healing

the healing community

sickness must lead to confession

not in the scriptures

1500 A.D.

danger of death

called Extreme Unction

1100 A.D.
1000 A.D.

anointing connected with last confession; consecrated for death

anointing only by priest or bishop

700 A.D.

sickness as God's punishment

healing the whole person

500 A.D.

influence of philosophy

312 A.D.

healings happening

blessed oil into homes

100 A.D.

Scriptural Roots

John 3:16-17 God so loved the world
Luke 5:16 Alone to pray
Mark 1:41 Healing touch
John 4:46-54 Words that give life
Philippians 2:6-11 Attitude of service
Matthew 14:14 Compassion of Jesus
Luke 17:11-19 Invitation to wholeness
Luke 8:40-56 Faith for salvation

Mark 10:46-52 Faith relationship
John 10:10 Life to the full
Luke 9:2 Apostles sent to heal
James 5:14-15 Anointing of the sick
Acts 3:4-7 Healing in Jesus' name
Acts 8:4-7 Healing
1 Corinthians 12:7-10 Healing as gift
John 15:12 Love one another

FIVE

Soaking in Healing Love— Anointing of the Sick

"Yes, God so loved the world
that he gave his only Son,
that whoever believes in him may not die
but may have eternal life.
God did not send the Son into the world
to condemn the world,
but that the world might be saved through
 him."

(John 3:16-17)

Scriptural Roots

God's great love that sent Jesus into the world is the life force of all creation and the essence of the Christian healing ministry. Jesus' healing ministry was an expression of this intense and unconditional love. Through his entire personality Jesus radiated that love, bringing wholeness to the physical, emotional and spiritual lives of all who were open to it. To all who loved in return he promised the ultimate healing of an eternal love relationship with him.

The sacrament of the anointing of the sick is meant to be the continuation of Jesus' healing ministry. It was originally intended to re-enact the healing love and personality of Jesus, to allow the sick to encounter his healing presence after he was no longer physically present on earth. Through the gathering of concerned people, the laying on of hands, the anointing with oil, and the prayers for health prayed in expectant faith, the early Christians sought to bathe the sick in the healing love of Jesus their Lord. Throughout history this sacrament deviated from its original intent, but in recent times it is being restored to its scriptural purpose. We shall journey into the scriptural roots to see what Jesus did and what we can do in his

71

name to anoint one another with his healing and peace.

I probably would never have examined the scriptural roots of healing so thoroughly if it had not been for the healing which I witnessed while studying theology in Innsbruck, Austria 13 years ago. Through my own experience of the Lord's love for me at that time in my life, I began going with a small group to the local hospital to sing religious music for those who were ill. One evening as we were singing a young man called us into his room and asked if we would pray for him to be healed. He had been in a body cast for nine weeks after a serious skiing accident, and the doctors said he would experience much pain and perhaps need therapy when they removed the cast. I could play a little guitar and sing a few songs, but I had never been asked to pray with someone for healing. I do not remember the words, but in some simple way we prayed that this young man would be healed and have no pain the next day when the cast was removed.

The next day, to our amazement, the man called us. He was very excited and asked us what we had done. He said the doctor "almost fainted" when after cutting off the cast he found that the patient could move his neck and shoulders freely without any pain. He said he had been up and down the elevator four times already because the doctors could not believe the X-rays which showed no damage from the accident.

What had we done? That incident, together with other healings in our prayer group, led me to search the scriptures to find out what Jesus had done to bring healing to so many. I pondered questions such as, Why don't more people pray for healing? What could I do to bring the good news of healing to the sick? Why did the sacrament which began as a continuation of Jesus' healing ministry became a sacrament ministered almost exclusively to the dying? This chapter reflects the insights I have gained through my study of Jesus' healing ministry and my own personal experience in that ministry.

If we journey through the gospels to see what Jesus did to heal people we find no consistent words or gestures. Sometimes he touched a person, sometimes not. Sometimes he gave a word of command, sometimes he did not. Sometimes he spoke about faith, sometimes he did not even imply that faith was necessary. What is consistent in Jesus' healing ministry however, is his intense love, his healing personality, his desire to bring the sick to wholeness. God so loved that he sent Jesus, and Jesus so loved that he healed. It was the natural result of his redemptive mission on earth. He came to give life, to bring salvation, wholeness and lasting peace by loving with the unconditional love flowing from the Father.

We can understand then why during his healing ministry "he often retired to deserted places and prayed" (Lk 5:16). He had to be in close communion with the Father in order that this divine love could flow consistently through his words, his gestures, his whole personality and bring healing. His "alone time" with the Father gave him the power to love even when love was not returned, to proclaim health when sickness seemed to have the upper hand, to proclaim life when death seemed to be in charge. His healing ministry was not so much doing the "right" thing, as being in union with the right one, the one who gives life.

This awareness made me realize that spending time alone with the Lord is essential to minister the healing love of God. It is the *presence* of God that we bring through our personality, our whole being, that touches the hearts of people and ministers healing. Our time spent absorbed in prayer not only empowers us to bring God's presence to the ill, but it also helps us discern in what ways we can best minister to those people the Lord puts on the road of life with us.

Jesus expressed his healing love in unique and personal ways to the people he met in order that each one could feel touched and affirmed in their deepest area of pain. For the alienated leper who felt untouchable, he used the gesture of touch to bring healing (Mk 1:41). For Peter's mother-in-law, the holding of her hand expressed his healing concern (Mk 1:31). For Zacchaeus who was bound up in fear, his gentle invitation to come down and his readiness to sit at table with him were the gestures of healing (Lk 19:1-10). For the royal official who understood the power of a spoken word of command, Jesus expressed his healing love in the simple words, "Return home. Your son will live" (Jn 4:50). As a minister of healing I find it very important to ask the Lord often, "How can I make this person to whom I am ministering feel loved with your love?" Any words, or readings, or actions that we use to bring healing must flow from that question.

Jesus' healing ministry flowed from his willingness to enter personally into people's suffering to let them know that they were lovable. His whole act of becoming a human being like us expressed this. He "emptied himself and took the form of a slave, being born in the likeness of men" (Phil 2:7) in order to demonstrate his great love and his desire to free us from the power of sin and illness. Jesus was moved at the very depth of his being when he saw people suffering from illness. St. Matthew writes that "his heart was moved with pity" when he saw the vast crowd on the shores of the Sea of Galilee, "and he cured their sick" (Mt 14:14). The Greek word used here and in other healing accounts which we translate as "moved with pity" is used exclusively in the gospels to express the intense divine love of Jesus and his desire to make people well. He entered into their pain with his whole being, not to commiserate with them, but rather to raise them from illness to wellness through his unconditional love for them. It is our own desire and readiness to enter into other people's pains with Jesus' love that allows healing to happen.

Jesus' healing ministry, by making people well, invited them to the eternal health for which God created them. It proclaimed in a visible way the eternal love of the Father, and the eternal love relationship that he wished to have with all people. This is the meaning of salvation. When people responded to his healing invitation with faith, Jesus let them know that they would have life forever. This is evident in his ministry to the ten lepers (Lk 17:11-19). The account tells us that on their way to show themselves to the priest, "they were cured." Jesus cleansed the skin of all ten, but to the one who came back in gratitude, he said, "your faith has been your salvation." The word used to refer to the ten tells us that they were physically healed, but the word used for the one who returned tells us that he will have eternal health, or salvation through his response of faith. He would never die.

The word used for "faith" here is not just an intellectual trust, like one would put in an airplane just before taking off, but rather, it means a faith-relationship, a readiness to interact with someone in trust. The one leper's physical cleansing led him to a unique relationship with Jesus that had eternal significance. I have seen people arrive at that kind of faith-relationship with God through healing prayer, even when they were not physically cured. They received the more significant healing.

This faith response to Jesus' healings is not spoken of in the gospels as necessary for physical cures. When present, however, it allows persons to see their healing as an invitation to stay in a close relationship with the Healer. Nowhere in the original Greek text of the gospel does it say, "your faith has 'cured' you." Rather, what it expresses is that to those who freely responded to Jesus' cures with an openness to keep on believing in him, he promised *salvation* or eternal health. We can see this in the healing of the woman with the hemorrhage (Lk 8:48), the raising of Jairus' daughter (Lk 8:50), and the healing of Bartimaeus (Mk 10:52). St. John expressed that same message when he wrote that God sent Jesus into the world "that whoever believes in him may not die but may have eternal life" (Jn 3:16). Through a faith-relationship with Jesus, we have a new vision of life, a vision that sees all things in light of God's eternal love.

Jesus' healing ministry was different from that of other healers of his time in that it always had this eternal goal in mind. He was concerned for the whole person. He wanted people to live knowing they were loved and that they could have life forever through him. Jesus could not force people to respond to his healing love with a desire to love in return. He simply continued to proclaim that God was in their midst loving them with a love that had eternal significance. The sacrament of anointing and indeed all forms of healing ministry are meant to do the same.

Jesus' ministry of healing not only invited people to eternal health, but clearly dispelled an Old Testament understanding that suffering from illness was God's way of punishing a sinner. We could hardly imagine that Jesus spent so much of his ministry healing people if his Father was somewhere up in heaven punishing people by making them sick. The unity and love between Jesus and the Father would make this impossible. The Godhead could not be divided that way. Life involves illness. Sometimes we make ourselves sick, sometimes others make us sick or cause injury, sometimes we do not fully understand the source of our sickness or injury, but through his ministry of healing, Jesus revealed himself as being on the side of health. He wants us to be well. The sacrament of anointing is a visible proclamation of that message.

We may search the gospels at times to try to understand the mystery of illness, suffering, and even death. Jesus offers no explanation for suffering, he simply offers a response to the person who is suffering; it is a response of love that flows from his entire being. Jesus did not heal everyone as we see in the scriptures. He must have watched his earthly father die, as well as some of his friends. His ministry of healing love and his message of salvation do proclaim however, that no illness is ultimate, no sickness is final, not even death can withstand the power of God's eternal love. That message gives us the peace of knowing that he is with us in those mysteries, loving us into wholeness and ultimately eternal life. It dispels our fears and feelings of alienation. It gives a deep underlying peace even when we do not understand the meaning of all that is happening.

Those who work with caring for the sick and suffering know that what such people often need, more than explanations, are loving arms to hold them and express the care of Jesus. Even if we could explain all the mysteries of human suffering, we would not be doing what Jesus did, namely, ministering to the one who is suffering. His ministry assures us that he is with us in pain. That assurance of his love often makes a person's body more susceptible to physical healing. This is evident in the observation that people who receive healing prayer before surgery and are at peace with the Lord generally heal faster and require less pain medication. As Christians we are called to proclaim that healing message by bathing the sick and suffering in the love of the Lord.

There were times in Christian history when the healing ministry was squelched by philosophies that taught that the physical body was supposed to suffer, and by theologies that resurrected the Old Testament idea that God punishes people by sending illness. We will see more on this in the history of the anointing sacrament. It is important that we realize that such teachings do not come from Jesus. Jesus is on the side of those who are ill, trying to love them into health.

At times people have misunderstood Jesus' words about "taking up your cross" to mean that he was encouraging people who were ill to keep on suffering. Jesus never did that. Yes, he did accept and even found meaning in the suffering that was part of his redemptive mission, and he taught his followers to do the same; but to those bound in the grip of illness, he offered his healing love and the message of salvation. People may put meaning in their suffering from illness or an accident, but the gospel tells us that Jesus wants them to be well, to be at peace, to "have life and have it to the full" (Jn 10:10). I know a number of people who are powerful ministers of healing even though their physical bodies are not in perfect health because they radiate such an inner joy and peace flowing from the Lord's love. They do not let their wounds or physical imperfections keep them from proclaiming the healing power of God's eternal love. They have found the peace of Jesus' healing love, and they share that peace with others.

The gospels tell us that Jesus commissioned his disciples to carry his healing message and his healing love to those in need. While he was still with them he sent them out to "proclaim the reign of God and heal the afflicted" (Lk 9:2). As a result of that sending, St. Mark records that "they expelled many demons, anointed the sick with oil, and worked many cures" (Mk 6:13). Jesus wanted his healing ministry to continue after he was gone and so he taught his followers how to bathe people in his love. The "power" he gave them to cure diseases was the power of love, the same power he radiated in his ministry while on earth.

After Jesus' death and resurrection, the early Christian communities continued his healing ministry in a number of ways. The letter of James indicates that this ministry was officially done by the presbyters or representatives of the church. We read,

> Is there anyone sick among you? He should ask for the presbyters of the church. They in turn are to pray over him, anointing him with oil in the Name of the Lord. This prayer uttered in faith will reclaim the one who is ill, and the Lord will restore him to health (Jas 5:14-15).

Through the gathering of these representatives of the church, their prayers, and the anointing in Jesus' name, the sick person was bathed in the healing presence of the Lord. The presbyters gathered to represent the whole community surrounding the ill person with love. The oil, which was the main healing agent of that time period, was ministered in the "Name of the Lord." This meant that it was intended to convey the whole *personality* of the Lord Jesus, all of the concern and care that he showed for the sick during his lifetime. The prayers uttered in faith expressed the expectance and the concern of all who were present as well as that of the whole community.

Here we see the origins of the sacrament of the anointing of the sick. It is meant to express the whole church's concern for the sick and their belief in the healing love of Jesus. It is the church's official expression of Jesus' healing ministry and like his ministry was always closely connected to the forgiveness of sins. For this reason the sacraments of reconciliation and anointing were often celebrated together.

The healing ministry of Jesus was not only continued in the church's official expression, but also flowed through those who radiated his healing presence in their individual lives. We read in the Acts of the Apostles, for example, how Peter and John ministered healing in Jesus' name to a crippled man at the temple gate (Acts 3:18), and how Philip preached and brought healing to many in Samaria (Acts 8:4-7). Paul not only ministered healing (Acts 14:8-10; 28:8-9) but he also wrote about it. His first letter to the Corinthians speaks of healing as a gift of the Spirit which when evident, was to be used out of love for the common good of the community (1 Cor 12:4-11). No matter how the healing ministry of Jesus was carried out after his resurrection, it was meant to proclaim his love and his ultimate gift of eternal life. It was not magic, nor was it a skill that deserved payment or a reward of honor. The Christian healing ministry is in its essence the *ministry of loving* as Jesus loved, a mission to which every Christian is called by Jesus who said,

This is my commandment:
love one another
as I have loved you" (Jn 15:12).

In summary, then, we have seen that Jesus was the fullest expression of the Father's great love and that he loved with an intensity and power that brought healing and peace. Healing was central to his mission of redemption. He came to bring wholeness and life. He entered into people's suffering from his whole being and radiated an unconditional love that flowed from his oneness with the Father. He clearly dispelled the idea that illness was a punishment from God and he proclaimed that no illness was ultimate, for God's love could break even the power of death. To all who responded to his healing love with a desire to continue a relationship with him, he promised entry into eternal life. Before he died, he commissioned his disciples to continue this healing ministry in his name. The members of the Christian community did this in an official way and through their personal spiritual lives.

As we have seen in earlier chapters, the healing love of Jesus continues to be expressed in some way through the sacraments of baptism, Eucharist, and reconciliation. The sacrament of the anointing of the sick, however, offers a unique occasion for the sick person to be bathed in the love of Jesus and the larger community through visible expressions that convey healing and the community's concern. This sacrament is a proclamation that God is with us in our illness, loving us into health of mind, body and soul. We will now examine how this sacrament developed through the years of history.

Historical Development

Written evidence from the early centuries of the church indicates that the healing power of Jesus remained present among his people. The early Fathers of the church during the first centuries refer to numerous healings happening through prayers in the name of Jesus. We recall that through baptism the members of these early Christian communities committed themselves to each other in a deep way and were dedicated to serving one another's needs. It is understandable then why the sick among them would have felt cared for with the love of Jesus and brought to wholeness in his name. These early Christians blessed the sick with Jesus' love while they ministered to their physical ailments with oil. Since oil was the main healing agent of that time, it became the natural symbol to express the healing care of the Lord.

In the early centuries there is evidence of two forms of anointing of the sick for healing. One was done by the bishop or priest and was related to the forgiveness of sins as well as healing. The other form which continued until the eighth century, was an anointing with oil done by relatives of the sick or even by the sick people themselves. The oil was always blessed in the name of the Lord by the bishop during the celebration of the Eucharist. People brought this oil to be blessed and then took it home with them and used it to anoint themselves or the sick among them as a symbol of the Lord's healing love. The anointing when done by the bishop or priest, was an expression of the total community's care for the ill person.

Copies of the prayers used by the bishop to bless the oil of anointing show us that the early Christians expected this sacrament to bring healing to the whole person, body, mind and spirit. This oil, blessed in Jesus' name, conveyed his presence and let people know that his healing love was surrounding them. It was used often and for any type of illness with the prayer that the person would be restored to full health.

During the fourth and fifth centuries however, the church's understanding of healing was significantly altered by the influence of Gnostic and Manichean philosophies. These philosophies downgraded the value of the physical body conveying the message that it was bad and not to be trusted. This influence eventually led the church to teach that physical healing was opposed to the ideal of Christianity. Christian leaders began warning people about putting too much attention on physical healing lest they lost their souls in the process. We can see how such ideas undercut Jesus' ministry of caring for the whole person and his desire to have them well. Physical healing was no longer understood as an invitation to eternal wholeness, but as a distraction from it. The healing message of Jesus gave way to un-Christian philosophies and it has taken until recent times to restore it.

By the late sixth century this influence had led to the understanding that bodily illness was one method used by God to punish his children for their sins. This Old Testament idea, which Jesus' ministry of healing had clearly dispelled, was now being taught by the leaders of his church. Through these developments in history the church had lost sight of Jesus' central healing message that he was *with* and not against the sick person, and that he desired to bring healing. The sick came to be treated with contempt rather than with the compassion of Jesus. Prayer for physical healing was no longer seen as advisable; in fact, it was suggested to be contrary to God's will, since illness was believed to be his way of "correcting" a sinner. It is understandable, then, why the sacrament of the anointing of the sick, originally intended to continue Jesus' healing ministry, gradually lost this emphasis on healing and began to focus almost exclusively on preparing a person for death.

I cringe inside. when I see sick people yet today still suffering under the influence of these ideas. They feel that God is against them in their illness. At the very time when they need to feel bathed in the healing love of Jesus, they doubt his central healing message and believe that they are meant to suffer in guilt or with a feeling of abandonment. I believe that through the restoration of Jesus' healing ministry and message within Christian communities, his deep peace and healing is being brought in a more powerful way to the sick and the suffering.

Gradually, during the eighth century, the anointing of the sick was no longer done by lay people. It came to be understood as a duty of the priests and bishops with the focus more and more on the healing of the soul. During the 800s an official rite of anointing was developed and it was closely associated with the sacrament of penance. It included a blessing with holy water, the laying on of hands, the anointing with oil on the five senses, and the praying of numerous prayers and psalms for healing and forgiveness of sins. The rite included the confessing of sins and the reception of the Eucharist.

Since the confessing of sins during this period came to be done just before death to minimize the length of the rigorous penances which were given for sins, the sacrament of the anointing, in conjunction with the sacrament of penance, came to be administered only to those who were at death's door. In this context the anointing of the sick gradually came to be understood as a consecration for death, rather than a sacrament for healing, and could be received only once. While it contained some of the healing actions of Jesus and a number of prayers for healing, it was listed as the "last rites" of a person's life and healing was not expected. We see, then, why by the 12th century it came to be called Extreme Unction, which means "last anointing," and healing was no longer understood to be one of its effects.

In this sense, the healing ministry of Jesus no longer had an official expression in the Western Christian church by the 12th century. Through the influence of philosophy and the connection with the sacrament of penance, this one-time sacrament for healing had become a blessing for death. Despite this development, however, records indicate that Christianity was never completely without healing experiences. The sacrament of anointing, even with its focus on the afterlife, still was at times the occasion for healings. Other sacraments which manifest the love of Jesus continued to bring about healings and inner peace. The healing power of Jesus' love continued to flow through the healing gifts and personalities of those who had a close relationship with him. Through their prayers and concern, healings occurred. This is evident in the life histories of those who came to be called saints.

From the 12th to the 16th centuries the church continued to seek to understand the ministry of healing and the effects of the sacrament of anointing. The healing effect of anointing was never denied, but it was not expected either. The theologians of this period sought to explain this phenomenon by focusing on the spiritual effects of this sacrament, emphasizing that it made a person ready for death. Through this emphasis, they gradually taught that a person *had* to be in danger of death in order to receive the sacrament. During this period they never questioned the underlying philosophical influences which caused Christians to doubt Jesus' desire and power to bring healing. Many explained his healings as actions he performed to show he was God, rather than realizing that they were expressions of his love as God and that he told his followers to love with the same kind of healing love. Christian leaders of this time continued to be suspicious of physical healing for the sick, lest the person not get their due "punishment" from God which they believed to be the purpose for the sickness.

The reformers of the 16th century questioned the practice of anointing the sick for death since it was not found in the scriptures. They denied that it was a true sacrament for this reason, but offered no more effective occasion for restoring people to health. The Council of Trent, in response to the reformers of this period, reaffirmed the sacramentality of Extreme Unction without searching into its scriptural or historical roots. It listed the effects of this sacrament as including the pardon of all sins and punishment due to sin, the strengthening of the sick person to carry the sickness and resist evil temptations, and physical healing when it was helpful to the person's salvation. It rejected the idea that only the dying could receive this sacrament but it still emphasized that the sacrament was meant primarily for the dangerously ill. While in words the Council of Trent opened the door for a broader use of the sacrament of Extreme Unction, the spirituality of that time period, plus the church's understanding of illness as a way of God bringing people to moral reform, kept this sacrament focused primarily on the dying. In practice this one-time healing sacrament continued until recent times to be administered almost exclusively to the dying as a last anointing in preparation for eternity.

Through the recent efforts of biblical scholars and the Second Vatican Council (1962-1965), this sacrament began to be restored to its original intent as seen in the scriptures. As a result its name changed from Extreme Unction to the anointing of the sick, indicating a new emphasis on the healing of the sick person. This sacrament is no longer limited to the dangerously ill. It was never meant to be, for Jesus lavished his healing love upon all the sick in hopes of bringing them wholeness in all areas of their lives. The sacrament of anointing is meant to be the community's expression of Jesus' compassion and care for the sick today. It is meant to let people know that in their illness God and the Christian community are with them, loving them into health. This is particularly important where a person is confined to a hospital or their home, separated from community activities. With this in mind, the new rite of anointing encourages members of the community to join the priest in bringing the healing presence of Jesus to the sick. All are called to bathe the sick in the presence of Jesus the Healer.

The oil blessed by the bishop and the presence of the priest at the anointing convey the prayers and love of not only the local community but also the universal church. This love and care was experienced by a Lutheran woman who mistakenly was anointed by a priest before surgery. She was not able to communicate her mistaken identity at the time, but afterward she would not have wanted to. She gave witness of the great peace that came over her through that sacrament. "Now I understand," she said, "the power of the prayer of the church."

I find that the most powerful healings happen when sick people feel totally surrounded in the love of Jesus evidenced by the prayers and concern of the people gathered around them. The reading of God's word, the laying on of concerned hands, the anointing with blessed oil, and the prayers for healing which are all part of the sacrament of anointing are powerful avenues for Jesus' presence to touch the lives of the sick and restore them to health of body, mind and soul. To all who are soaked in this healing encounter, something always happens.

Soaking people in the healing love of Jesus is not limited to the sacrament of anointing. As we have seen, the ministry of healing is essentially the ministry of loving. We all can give visible form to that love through our visits to the sick, our touch, our prayers with them. The Catholic church has again opened the way for those who care for the sick to express their healing concern through the use of blessed oil. In all of these ways, the healing ministry of Jesus is continued.

The sacrament of anointing in its revised form uses all of these avenues to bathe the sick as a total church community in the healing presence of Jesus. The healing Masses which I mentioned in chapter three combine the healing actions of this sacrament with the healing power of Jesus' presence in the Eucharist. Many have found these Masses to be very powerful experiences of Jesus' healing presence. Through the receiving of Jesus in the Eucharist as a community and the specific care and prayers for those seeking wholeness, we have witnessed many physical, emotional and spiritual healings. People who come consistently speak about the healing love of Jesus that they feel during those celebrations.

Despite the fact that the sacrament of anointing deviated from its original intent through history, it did at times occasion healings. This fact reminds us of the mystery of sacraments, the mystery of God's free, healing love poured out upon his people in many different ways. It is our calling as Christians, however, to minister God's healing love as powerfully as we can using the example of Jesus, and then to let the mystery of his love bring about his will. We will never answer all the questions about the mystery of illness, suffering and healing. We're not called to answer all the questions, but we are called and commissioned by our baptism to seek ways of bathing the sick in the presence of the Healer, and then to leave the results in his hands. This challenge is not just for the leaders of the church, but for every Christian. Jesus' words and life example call us to minister healing to the extent that our gifts allow.

I believe that as the healing power of the praying church continues to be felt, the sacrament of anointing will grow in use and expectancy among all the Christian churches. It seems only appropriate that the healing ministry which was so dear to Jesus' heart would not be limited by un-Christian philosophies or divided theologies. It is our Christian challenge to let that love so radiate through our personalities, our actions, and our prayers that the sick among us experience healing and true peace. God so loved the world that he sent Jesus. Jesus so loved that he healed. We as Christians must so manifest his love that those who are ill feel soaked in the love that gives life.

MARRIAGE

Historical Development

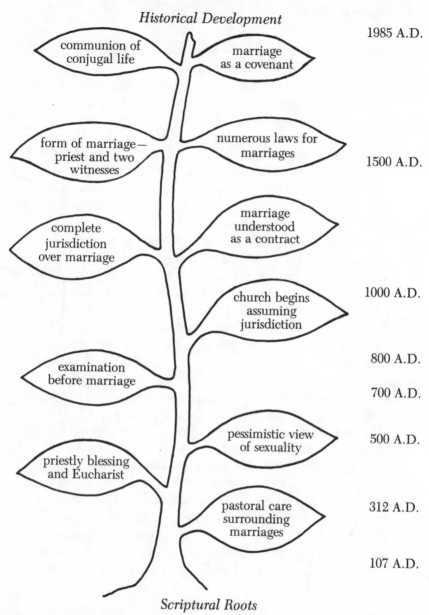

communion of conjugal life

marriage as a covenant

1985 A.D.

form of marriage— priest and two witnesses

numerous laws for marriages

1500 A.D.

complete jurisdiction over marriage

marriage understood as a contract

church begins assuming jurisdiction

1000 A.D.

800 A.D.

700 A.D.

examination before marriage

pessimistic view of sexuality

500 A.D.

priestly blessing and Eucharist

pastoral care surrounding marriages

312 A.D.

107 A.D.

Scriptural Roots

Matthew 19:3-6 Sacredness of marriage
Genesis 2:18, 24 Two become one
Hosea 1:1-3:5 Faithfulness as a sign
Isaiah 54:5-8 Image of enduring love
Mark 10:6-9 Permanence of marriage
Matthew 19:10 Uniqueness of Jesus' words
Matthew 19:9 Later provision added

1 Corinthians 7:12-14
   Union consecrated by God
Mark 10:11-12 Equal responsibility
1 Corinthians 7:3-4 Equality in marriage
Ephesians 5:25 Marriage as a witness
1 Timothy 4:1-4 Marriage as good
John 2:1-11 Jesus affirms marriage

SIX

Surrounding the Two With Care—Marriage

Jesus replied, "Have you not read that at the beginning the Creator made them male and fe-
male and declared, 'For this reason a man shall
leave his father and mother and cling to his
wife, and the two shall become as one'? Thus
they are no longer two but one flesh."

(Matthew 19:4-6)

Scriptural Roots

The sacrament of marriage is not based on the
actions of Jesus as the other sacraments are, but rather it
originates from his attitude toward marriage. Jesus did
not "perform" marriages, nor did he directly commission
his disciples to perform them, but he left his followers an
attitude toward marriage which made it a sacred reality,
a sign of the power of God's love. The Christian community felt the need to preserve his attitude affirming the sacredness of marriage and to surround the marriages of
their members with special care.

Jesus says precious little about marriage, but his few
words root the sacredness of marriage in the story of creation (Gn 2:18-24). His words tell us that in the Father's
original plan the two bound in the union of marriage
were to "become one," and when that union was formed
in him, it must remain as a sign of his faithful enduring
love. It is Jesus' attitude about the permanence of marriage as a sacred sign of divine love that forms the basis
for understanding marriage as a sacrament.

Jesus' concern for faithfulness in marriage moved the
Christian community to surround marrying couples with

care and the blessings of the Lord. From early on the community's care was meant to help the marrying couple encounter the love of the risen Lord as they began their life together. Christian couples continued to marry according to the customs of their time, but because of their relationship with the Lord, their union of committed love became a living witness of God's faithful love for his people. Their life of faithful love became a living sacrament, an ongoing sign of the presence and power of God's love.

The witness value of marriage is rooted not only in the New Testament, but also in the Old Testament writings. From the story of creation we see that marriage was understood as good and part of God's plan of salvation. Gradually through the prophets it began to be given a religious significance. The prophet Hosea was the first to speak of marriage as an image of God's faithful love for his people. His words came at a time when the chosen people were being unfaithful to their Creator. God called Hosea to be faithful and forgiving to his unfaithful wife as a symbol to the people of how God himself is always faithful in love to his people (Hos 1:1-3:5). Isaiah the prophet continued that same image, expressing God's love for his chosen people as the enduring love of a husband for his wife (Is 54:5-8). Through God's words spoken by the prophets, the Old Testament people came to believe that marriage was a sacred union imaging God's faithfulness and therefore was not to be dissolved without a very serious reason.

The Jewish rabbis of Jesus' time, while they believed in the value of a faithful witness in marriage, each had his own conditions which were taught as adequate grounds for divorce. Since these conditions varied greatly, the Pharisees came to ask Jesus what *he* would consider grounds for a decree of divorce. It is in this context that "some Pharisees came up and as a test began to ask him whether it was permissible for a husband to divorce his wife" (Mk 10:2 or Mt 19:3). Unique from all others of his

time, and unprecedented in Jewish history, Jesus affirms
the absolute indissolubility of marriage with his response,

> "At the beginning of creation God made them
> male and female; for this reason a man shall
> leave his father and mother and the two shall
> become as one. They are no longer two but one
> flesh. Therefore let no man separate what God
> has joined" (Mk 10:6-9).

Jesus did not believe that marriage bonds were to be
dissolved or broken. His unique teaching took marriage
beyond the laws taught by Moses (Dt 23:1-4) and put it in
the realm of God's creative plan. He reveals a perspective
of marriage that is more than just two people joining
themselves to each other. His teaching is based on the
power of God to mold two people into one. It is *God's*
joining of two people that makes Christian marriage
unique and able to be a sign of his eternal love. It is God's
love perfecting the human love existing between two people that allows them to stand out as a witness of faithfulness for the community. In Jesus' view there are no adequate grounds for breaking such a union.

Jesus' words on marriage were unprecedented in Jewish history and the rest of the ancient world. The disciples'
surprise and question concerning his words (Mt 19:10)
make us aware that no one had ever taught about marriage quite like this before. They would not have reacted
that way if his words were not so unique and absolute.

Jesus stresses the holiness and the preciousness of
marriages that are joined together in God's love. He is not
saying that every marriage is indissoluble, but only those
that are "joined by God." He says nothing about marriages
that are not joined and united in the love of God.

I do not think that being joined by God was meant
to refer only to exchanging marriage vows in church.
Marriage as a living, growing relationship needs to be
joined daily by the forgiving and healing love of God. Statistics I heard some time ago about marriages in the

United States indicate the power of consistently focusing on Christ as the center of the marriage. They show that in our country, 50 out of 100 nonreligious marriages end in divorce; 33 out of 100 religious marriages end in divorce; ten out of 100 marriages in which couples worship together end in divorce; and only one out of 1105 marriages in which couples pray *with* each other on a daily basis ends up in divorce. These statistics make it obvious that God's presence consistently invited into the marriage union is very significant in keeping the couple in unity.

Faithfulness and consistent care for another person in any form of Christian friendship requires a deep personal union with the Lord, and a commitment to exemplify the values he proclaimed. His words on marriage were truly a challenge to all who heard them and they remain so to all who seek to live faithfully in their marriages. The effort and sacrifices involved in making his love central in marriages and in any Christian friendship become a hymn of praise to the honor of his name.

As we look at the two scriptural accounts of Jesus' unprecedented words on marriage and divorce (Mk 10:2-12 and Mt 19:3-9), we notice that in the latter account there is an exception mentioned for which a marriage could be dissolved. Since Mark's account contains the more original version of Jesus' words on the permanence of marriage, it becomes evident that by the time Matthew wrote his gospel the early community was questioning whether there might be a valid reason for a husband or wife to divorce his or her spouse. In Matthew's account of Jesus' words concerning divorce, the phrase "lewd conduct is a separate case" (Mt 19:9) was added. It is very difficult to know exactly what this phrase could have meant to the early church. It does indicate, however, that from early on the followers of Jesus wrestled with his absolute words on the permanence of marriage and struggled to live up to his ideal.

As we have seen, Jesus spoke of the permanence of

marriage only in cases where God's divine love was continually forming and fashioning the union. In reality the Christian community recognized that such was not always the case, and thus they struggled to discover Jesus' intent in less-than-ideal situations. This struggle over divorce and remarriage has caused much pain and alienation throughout Christian history, with various Christian denominations suggesting different solutions. No solution seems to resolve the tension between Jesus' unique words on the permanence of marriage and his numerous words on forgiveness and reconciliation. We can not erase his words. Perhaps we must continue to live with the tension, seeking to uphold both values by our care and concern for marriages and our understanding of those who, despite all their efforts, have not been able to let God join them in a permanent bond of love.

No matter how the various churches resolve the issue of divorce, Jesus' words on the permanence of marriage remain. He spoke of this permanence of marriage as the original intent of his Father. Though the prophets had spoken of marriage as an example of God's faithful love, they had never rooted its witness value so strongly in God's original plan of creation. It seems that Jesus was aware not only of the witness value of marriage for the community but also of the need for children to be created and nurtured in the environment of masculine and feminine love. My work in the healing ministry makes me aware of how important it is for both complementary forms of love to be present as children grow. Parents have a unique opportunity and responsibility to let the love of God flow through them to their children. A marriage joined in God's love gives a profound witness to the children of that union.

We get an idea of the early church's understanding of marriage from Paul's words to the Corinthian community (1 Cor 7:12-14). In this letter he indicates his belief that married life is transformed into a sacred union by the two people's individual love relationship with the Lord. He points out that even if one partner in the marriage is not Christian, the love of God can center that union through the "believing" spouse and make it a "consecrated" and holy union. It is the intimacy of the union that allows the love of God to flow through the believing spouse, consecrating the unbelieving spouse and the children.

It is important to point out that both Jesus and Paul affirm the equality of men and women in the marriage relationship. Jesus' words on marriage denied the teaching of his Jewish heritage that the wife was the property or possession of the husband. Against the cultural understanding of his time, Jesus says that husbands and wives each have equal responsibility to be faithful and self-giving in marriage. He told his disciples, "Whoever divorces his wife and marries another commits adultery against her; and the woman who divorces her husband and marries another commits adultery" (Mk 10:11-12). In a similar way, Paul stressed that the obligations of marriage are to be shared on an equal basis. He writes, "The husband should fulfill his conjugal obligations toward his wife, the wife toward her husband. A wife does not belong to herself but to her husband; equally, a husband does not belong to himself but to his wife (1 Cor 7:3-4). This does not necessarily mean that the husband and wife do the same things, but rather that they respect each other equally in their unique roles. It is in the affirming of each other in their unique gifts that they give life to one another, to their family, and to their community.

Paul's words on husbands and wives relating to one another in his letters to the Colossians and Ephesians (Col 3:18-19 and Eph 5:22-33) can be confusing when taken out of their historical context. Since society at his time did not expect women to express love, he does not ask it of them as he does of men. His call for wives to be "loyal to their husbands" and husbands to "love their wives" is equally demanding and only possible on the basis of their marriage being founded "in the Lord." Both are challenged to model themselves on the self-sacrificing love of Christ.

In that same letter to the Ephesians (Eph 5:25), Paul expresses his view that Christian marriage was to be an example of Christ's love for his church. These words, like the words of the prophets, affirm the witness value of two people who faithfully love one another in marriage. His teaching makes us aware that Christians entering the sacrament of marriage do so not just for themselves, but they also commit themselves to be witnesses for their children and the community of how much God loves his people. They are to be living sacraments, living signs of enduring love so that their witness will bring many others to know that they are loved by God.

All the words of scripture regarding marriage affirm its goodness and the significance it has for the community. Jesus' presence at the wedding in Cana (Jn 2:1-11) together with his words regarding the sacredness of the marriage commitment express his affirmation of marriage as part of God's plan. Besides the words of Paul already mentioned, his words to Timothy (1 Tm 4:1-5) reaffirm his teaching on the goodness of marriage and criticize those who forbade marriages. His words, like Jesus', express the need for marriages to be joined and made holy by God through prayer. Such marriages according to their views must not be divided.

Marriage during New Testament times remained a civil event, but it was experienced by Christians in union with the Lord. Though they continued to marry according to the civil customs, a Christian couple knew that their marriage was more than just the joining of themselves to another person. Their commitment to Jesus made their commitment to each other a sacred reality, symbolizing his faithful, enduring love.

There are only a few precious words of Jesus on marriage but their absolute quality gave his followers a great challenge. His words gave marriage an eternal witness value and led the church to give special care to those seeking to live that permanent witness of love. The concern of the total Christian community to preserve Jesus' unique attitude toward marriage became the roots of what we call the sacrament of marriage. We shall see how this desire to surround marrying couples with care developed through the years of history.

Historical Development

Christian marriages in the first two centuries of the church were not performed any differently than other marriages; couples followed the civil customs of their culture to celebrate the beginning of their marriage. In their hearts however, they knew that their commitment was for life and carried the significance of witnessing to God's faithful love.

A letter of Ignatius dating back to A.D.107 told Christians that it would be fitting for those entering marriage to do so with the advice of their bishop. This document indicates the early church's desire to give special care and counsel to Christian couples who wished to enter marriage. This was not mandatory but simply an expression of the community's concern in helping a couple root their marriage in the Lord.

During these early centuries the marriage of a Christian to a pagan was condemned by the church. This flows from the great stress these early Christians put on their baptismal commitment. In baptism they "turned away" from pagan ways, and the church felt that by marrying a pagan they would be relinquishing their commitment. From Paul's letter to the Corinthians (1 Cor 7:12-16) we can understand that if a pagan was married to a pagan and became a Christian, he or she could remain married as long as they could live in peace. The first commitment made by a person took precedent over the second.

By the fourth century there is evidence of a priestly

blessing and prayers being part of the Christian marriages ceremony. This developed from the practice of the priest or bishop going to congratulate the couple after the wedding ceremony. The marriage ceremony at this time consisted of the father handing the bride over to her husband and the husband taking her into his home. It was the concern of the church leaders to bless those who were beginning married life that developed into the marriage sacrament. It was the couple's desire to have Christ be central in their marriage that made their marriage a sacrament for life.

Already at the time in Rome, the marriages of two baptized Christians were sealed by the celebration of the Eucharist as well as a blessing. Here we see the origins of what we celebrate as a wedding Mass, even though at this time there was not yet a verbal exchange of marriage vows. The Eucharist and the blessing which followed the marriage ceremony indicated to the whole community the holiness of marriage and the church's desire to help married couples live their new commitment faithfully and for life.

This celebration of the Eucharist and the giving of a blessing in the marriage ceremony was not obligatory. In fact, it was forbidden to those who did not live a good Christian life. It was not a law nor a necessary requirement to receive the blessing of the church but rather a *privilege* signifying the good example of the couple and the community's desire to affirm that good example. This understanding of the marriage blessing is very much in keeping with the scriptures and perhaps needs to be restored in our day. It might help us realize that asking for the sacrament of marriage is a commitment to be a sacramental witness.

During the eighth century Boniface made it obligatory for couples to be examined before marriage to determine if they were ready to live out their commitment. If they were not ready, or if they were living together before marriage, they could receive no blessing from the church. Again in this requirement we see the church's concern to help marrying couples build a life together founded on the values and the love of Christ.

During the ninth century the church began assuming juridical power over marriages, which means its leaders assumed the power to decide who was able to be married, and began performing the actual marriage ceremony. The Christian leaders saw the need to guard the sacredness of marriage in this way, since the Roman state which previously regulated marriages was collapsing. This concern to give pastoral care to marriages led to many ramifications causing the church to make numerous statements and laws about marriage.

By the 12th century the church had complete jurisdiction over marriage and sought to define what really constitutes a valid Christian marriage. Until this time, the validity of marriage depended only on the mutual consent of two baptized Christians. This led to the problem of numerous secret marriages. As the church tried to rectify this difficulty and define what was necessary for a valid marriage, it ended up developing many detailed laws. It seems that the church never intended to have such total jurisdiction over marriage, but rather was simply trying to ensure that its members lived their marriage commitments in keeping with the words and attitudes of Jesus. What began as the church's concern to protect the sacredness of marriage developed into a large legal structure which continues to govern marriage even today.

During the 12th century marriage came to be called an official sacrament since it was a permanent sign of God's enduring love. It did not continue an action of Jesus, as some of the other sacraments, but it preserved his attitude about the sacredness of marriage. It was understood that the couple administered the sacrament to each other through their promises of faithful love, recognizing that they were also promising to be a sign of the Lord's enduring love. The celebration of the Eucharist and the blessing for newly married couples became more and more a part of this exchange of vows, but it was not yet considered mandatory.

Part of the struggle to define the essence of marriage at this period in history led the Roman Catholic church to speak of marriage as a *contract* between two people in which they exchange "exclusive and perpetual rights" to beget children. This reflects a rather limited and pessimistic view of sex going back to the time of Augustine (c.400). The understanding of marriage as a contract helped clarify the boundaries of a valid marriage, but it minimized the fact that marriage is an ongoing relationship in which two people need to give of themselves to each other continually in heart, mind and body.

In the renewal of its understanding of marriage since the Second Vatican Council, the Catholic church began refering to marriage as a *covenant* rather than a contract between two people. The concept of marriage as a covenant accents the reality that a marriage relationship is never complete but requires the consistent giving of oneself to the other as well as the consistent inviting of God's love into the human exchange of love. It broadens the understanding of the sacrament of marriage to include not only the moment two people exchange their vows, but also the many moments when they offer the presence of Christ to one another in the exchanges of love and care.

During the 16th century the reformers denied that marriage was a sacrament, though they upheld the sacredness of marriage. The Catholic church reaffirmed the sacramentality of marriage since it was an effective, saving sign of God's love. The reformers also rejected the Catholic church's authority or jurisdiction over marriage, believing that such authority belonged to the civil government. As we saw, the church had assumed that authority when the Roman state was not doing it, and only did so to protect the sacredness of marriage. Perhaps it could have relinquished its jurisdiction over marriage at this time, but it chose not to and in the 1560s at the Council of Trent it reaffirmed its authority and jurisdictional power over marriage.

The church's concern to stop secret marriages and to protect the sacredness of marriage led to more laws regarding what constituted a valid marriage. The most significant of these laws was the church's rule of 1564 that the marriage of any baptized Catholic must take place before a priest and two witnesses. Once this form of marriage was set, all civil marriages by baptized Catholics were considered invalid. This law helped end secret marriages, but it became a source of great pressure for every Catholic marriage to be performed in a church before a priest, even when the couple involved were not committed, practicing Catholics. The marriage blessing moved from being an affirmation of a good witness and a sign of the community's care to a necessity for the validity of the marriage.

The time of the Reformation also raised the issue of divorce and remarriage. The reformers of the 16th century approved the practice of divorce as the "lesser of two evils" and allowed for remarriage of divorced people. The Catholic church, in its attempt to preserve Jesus' words on the permanence of the marriage sacrament, spent its efforts determining whether or not a marriage that failed was truly a valid sacramental marriage. If it found the marriage to be nonsacramental because some essential element for validity was missing, it declared the marriage null and allowed the person to enter a true sacramental marriage. This declaration of nullity or annulment is a recognition by the church that there was a marriage, but that it was nonsacramental because some essential part to making it sacramental was missing.

Obviously these declarations of nullity involve much analysis and many fine distinctions, which can cause some misunderstandings and questions at times. As marriage began to be defined more as a covenant relationship than a contract, it became even less clear as to whether a sacramental marriage ever existed or when it may have ended. It is important to realize that the intent of this annulment procedure is meant to help preserve the sacredness of the marriage commitment and to aid a person whose marriage failed to be reconciled with the Christian community and find peace within themselves. We might question the Catholic church's annulment process, but we must realize that no other Christian church puts more time and effort into preserving the sacredness of the marriage commitment as Jesus affirmed it than the Catholic church does. It would be much easier to do nothing.

The church's concern to surround marriages with pastoral care, from the 1500s onward, focused primarily on clarifying the laws of marriage, determining what were valid and invalid marriages. By the 20th century theologians started raising questions about marriage being called a contract with "rights" and "duties" to be performed by the couple. While such terminology had been useful in determining which marriages were valid or invalid, it did not speak to the relational, developing aspects of marriages. Gradually more and more church leaders began defining marriage as a covenant until, as mentioned before, the Vatican Council finally defined marriage as a "conjugal covenant of irrevocable personal consent."

This recent definition of marriage puts much more emphasis on the need to help the marrying couple develop the skills and the spirituality necessary to sustain an ongoing, life-giving union. It is a recognition that the marriage needs to be continually nurtured by the couple and by the affirmation of the community if they are to remain a sign of God's enduring love for his people. The church's concern to help couples establish a lasting covenant of love in the Lord is evidenced in its recent creation of marriage preparation programs.

The Pre-Marriage Inventories and marriage preparation classes are a service of love to the couples and a sign of the Christian community's care for them. Such preparation programs are a sign that the church is trying to take seriously its responsibility to preserve the sacredness of marriage and to surround the couple with pastoral care. It is out of *love* for the couples that the church puts so much effort into preparation for marriage, even at times when it is not experienced as such. It is not always easy to challenge couples to recognize the commitment they are about to make and to instruct them in the skills and spirituality necessary to sustain that life commitment, but it is the responsibility of the church community to do so. It is comforting to realize that these preparations are a great source of help to those sincerely seeking to enter a permanent love relationship in the Lord.

As Christians we are challenged to affirm and preserve the sacredness of marriage, especially in these times when the breakup of marriages is so evident. Now, more than ever, it is necessary as a community to surround marrying couples with spiritual care and adequate preparation for their life ahead. It is equally necessary to affirm those living out their marriage covenants by encouraging them in their faithfulness and enriching them in the skills needed to grow in their covenant of love. In a similar attitude of care, it is necessary continually to seek ways to reconcile and heal the wounds of broken marriages by helping people understand and grow beyond the mistakes of the past.

Much more could be written on the legal aspects of marriage and the church's way of dealing with divorce and remarriage. As a church community we need always to seek the truth in those very complex issues. What I have written is meant to help us understand Jesus' attitude toward marriage and the church's attempts to live in harmony with his teachings on that sacrament. As we have seen, Jesus said very little about marriage, but his words gave it a sacredness and a significance unknown before his time. All our efforts to keep his words alive, even though imperfect, are an expression of our desire to follow him and an indication of how much we long for true, visible signs of his faithful, enduring love for us. To all who give of themselves to preserve and affirm the faithful witness of committed love in our communities, we can be forever grateful. They are the living sacraments that point to the true Sacrament of Love.

HOLY ORDERS
Historical Development

1985 A.D.

lay ministries

enabling and ordering the gifts of all

establish seminaries

priesthood of all believers

1500 A.D.

decline in spiritual ministry

celibacy

investment of power

reform of papacy by Gregory VII

East separates from West

1100 A.D.

1000 A.D.

much missionary activity

intermingle royalty and spiritual leadership

priests increase, deacons decrease

500 A.D.

bishops chosen by bishops

bishops, priests and deacons

312 A.D.

develop more cultic priesthood

100 A.D.

Scriptural Roots

Ephesians 4:11-12 Enabling all to serve
John 13:4-15 Servant leaders
John 17:9-19 Prayer of consecration
Acts 2:14 Peter as spokesman
Acts 2:42 Apostles respected
Acts 8:14-17, 25 Prayer and preaching
Acts 15:2-29 Council of Jerusalem
Acts 11:22-26 Encouraged and instructed

Acts 14:21-23 Installed presbyters
1 Timothy 3:1-7 Presbyter – bishops
Romans 16:1-2 Deaconess
Acts 6:6 Laying on of hands
2 Timothy 1:6 Laying on of hands
Acts 13:3 Community empowerment
1 Peter 2:9 Priesthood of all
1 Corinthians 4:1 Administer God's mysteries

SEVEN

Equipping the Saints for Ministry—Holy Orders

It is he (Christ) who gave apostles, prophets, evangelists, pastors and teachers in roles of service for the faithful to build up the body of Christ.

(Ephesians 4:11-12)

Scriptural Roots

Leadership within the Christian community was a necessity after Jesus ascended to the Father. Someone had to direct and guide the mission of spreading the good news entrusted to the followers of Jesus. It was only natural for the apostles to fill that role initially but as time went on, the community had to establish a structure for selecting and affirming leadership so that the gifts in the community could be ordered and encouraged. It is this need for ongoing leadership that is the basis for the sacrament of holy orders.

During his time on earth, Jesus spoke in a very unique way about roles in leadership. He told his potential leaders that they could not lord it over people in their care, but that they "must serve the needs of all" (Mk 10:42-45). Jesus' whole life example in ministry proclaimed this vision of leadership. His entire life was a model of service, always seeking to minister to the needs of his people.

One of the final gestures of his life on earth proclaimed his unique attitude about leadership. During the final meal with his disciples, Jesus "rose from the meal and took off his cloak. He picked up a towel and tied it around himself. Then he poured water into a basin and began to wash his disciples' feet..." (Jn 13:4-5). In order that his disciples not miss the significance of this gesture Jesus said to them,

> "You address me as 'Teacher' and 'Lord,'
> and fittingly enough,
> for that is what I am.
> But if I washed your feet —
> I who am Teacher and Lord —
> then you must wash each other's feet. . .
> as I have done, so you must do" (Jn 13:13-15).

He taught his apostles and all who would follow him that those who led in his name, had to lead as *servants*. As servant leaders they would proclaim his presence.

Because Jesus knew that his apostles would face many challenges, he prayed for them in their ministry of leadership and "consecrated" himself as a source of strength and protection for their work. At the final meal with his apostles, Jesus addressed the Father in the following words:

> "For these I pray —
> not for the world
> but for these you have given me, . . .
> O Father most holy,
> protect them with your name which you have
>   given me
> that they may be one, even as we are one. . . .
> I gave them your word,
> and the world has hated them for it; . . .
> I do not ask you to take them out of the world,
> but to guard them from the evil one.
> . . . Consecrate them by means of truth —
> 'Your word is truth.'
> As you have sent me into the world,
> so I have sent them into the world;
> I consecrate myself for their sakes now,
> that they may be consecrated in truth" (Jn
>   17:9-19).

This is truly a beautiful prayer of "ordination," a prayer of consecration for all who accept the role of being leaders in the Christian community. It tells us that Jesus wished the leaders of his church to remain under his protection. As he protected his apostles during his life, he would offer his protection to his leaders forever. He dedicated himself to be their source of truth to guide them as they would go forth to teach in his name and guard the message of faith. In this prayer we see the origins of ordination. It is an expression of Jesus' desire to encircle his leaders with the power of his presence that they might serve the Father as he had served the Father. It remains a great source of affirmation to all who commit themselves to leadership in his church.

The New Testament does not leave us an organized blueprint for the sacrament of holy orders, but it indicates how the apostles and disciples of Jesus began to develop a system of structured leadership to guide the Christian community. The Acts of the Apostles (2:14) indicates that from early on Peter was the spokesman for the apostles. This leadership role seems to stem from Jesus' words to Peter at Caesarea Philippi telling him that he was the "Rock" on which he would build his church (Mt 16:13-20). It is on the basis of these words that the church established a primary position of leadership, which today we know as the pope. Someone needed to carry on this main leadership role and Peter was the first to do so.

We see in the Acts of the Apostles (2:42) that all the apostles were respected as instructors and leaders. As people who had listened often to Jesus' teachings and watched his actions, they were listened to and respected. When it became evident that they could not handle all the work of ministry, they selected deacons to take care of the additional physical needs of the community in order that they might be permitted "to concentrate on prayer and the ministry of the word" (Acts 6:4). They saw their main role as leaders of prayer and ministers of Jesus' words.

This was also evident in Samaria where Peter and John were sent after they heard about the word of God being accepted there: "The two went down to these people and prayed that they might receive the Holy Spirit.... After giving their testimony and proclaiming the word of the Lord, they went back to Jerusalem bringing the good news to many villages of Samaria on the way" (Acts 8:15,25). These accounts show us the primary role of the apostles and of all who represent their leadership roles today.

Besides being leaders in prayer and the ministry of the word, the apostles were respected as sources of unity. When the question of circumcision for non-Jewish Christians was raised, for example, and caused dissension in the community at Antioch, Paul and Barnabas with some others of that community went "to see the apostles and presbyters in Jerusalem about this question" (Acts 15:2). We see in this first council of the church the respect that is given to Peter and the apostles as sources of true teaching and unity. Their successors carried that same responsibility throughout history, even as they do in our day.

This account of the first church council outlines the original method used by the church leaders to resolve significant questions regarding Christian teachings. It can help us understand why throughout history councils were called to gather the church leaders in order to discern direction and to seek unity for the total church. We have noted throughout the significance of the Second Vatican Council (1962-1965) in this regard.

In addition to the apostles, there is evidence of other leaders in the New Testament who instructed, baptized, healed and encouraged the people who sought to know the Lord. In the Acts of the Apostles we read how Philip's ministry in Samaria was anointed with many healings and led many people to baptism (8:4-13). We read as well how Barnabas "encouraged the community at Antioch to remain firm in their commitment to the Lord" and "instructed great numbers" in their Christian faith (Acts 11:22-26). In a similar way, the letters of Paul tell us that during his missionary journeys he spent much of his time teaching, healing and encouraging the people he met.

The New Testament refers to a number of leadership positions that developed early in the church as the need for these positions arose. When Paul and Barnabas established Christian communities in various towns, for example, they "installed presbyters" (Acts 14:23) in each community to watch over the faith life of the people. Later Paul left Titus on the island of Crete that he might "accomplish what had been left undone, especially the appointment of presbyters in every town" (Ti 1:5). In referring to the people in these positions, Paul used the title presbyter and bishop interchangeably. The position or role of Presbyter-bishop was created to guard the faith life of the community members and, as such, the people in these roles could be considered successors to the apostles in a broad sense. They were to be the source of instruction, order and unity for the members of the communities in their care. The qualities which Paul saw as significant for this position are described in his first letter to Timothy (3:1-7) and his letter to Titus (1:6-9).

Deacons were seen as assistants to these leaders in areas of instruction and caring for the physical needs of the people. As we saw, the apostles saw fit to select seven men as deacons to distribute food to the needy. Their roles were not limited to that, however. Later we see Stephen (Acts 6:8-10) and Philip (Acts 8:4-13) preaching and healing. The order of diaconate developed as the needs of the church grew and was affirmed as a position of leadership by the apostles. There is evidence in Paul's letter to the Romans that the diaconate was shared in by women as well as men (Rom 16:1-2).

It is the offices of presbyter-bishop and deacon that emerge as the official leadership positions in the New Testament church. Two centuries later the office of priest was distinguished as an extension of the bishop. These three offices of *bishop, priest,* and *deacon* eventually became the focus of what we know as the sacrament of holy orders. It is interesting that when new roles of leadership developed after this as extensions of the bishop, the sacrament of holy orders was not used to affirm or ordain the people in those roles.

The New Testament portrays no rite of ordination as we have it today. Jesus, for example, after instructing his apostles, simply sends them out with his authority to minister in his name (Mk 6:7-13). Before his death as we saw, he prayed for them in the ministry of leadership, but he used no gesture to empower them, except the gesture of washing their feet, lest they forget that their role as leaders was one of servants.

There is evidence that after Jesus' ascension, the early church used the gesture of laying on hands as a way of affirming or ordaining leaders. The apostles in commissioning the seven deacons for their ministry "prayed over them and then imposed hands on them" (Acts 6:6). Paul also used the gesture of laying on of hands as a way of installing Timothy (2 Tm 1:6) and presumably other presbyters for their roles of leadership. This action conveyed not only a sense of empowerment for ministry, but also a sense of support and unity with those who performed it. It is interesting to note that at one point the community at Antioch gathered around their leaders Barnabas and Saul, and after fasting and praying, "imposed hands on them and sent them off" for their ministry to other communities (Acts 13:3). Here we see that the role of all the baptized to affirm leadership in the church is as significant as the role of the ordained leaders to do so. All have the power and responsibility to support and empower those called to leadership in the church.

The laying on of hands can be a beautiful expression of the community's desire to fulfill the role of affirming leadership in the church. I have personally felt the power of that gesture and the support which it conveys. The affirmation I experienced as the bishop and almost 100 priests one by one laid their hands on my head at ordination gave me a great sense of being loved and empowered as I entered my new role as priest for the Christian community. The day I left Innsbruck, Austria, to continue my study for ministry in the United States, the prayer community which I had led laid their hands on my head as a sign of their appreciation and as a gesture of support and empowerment for the ministry that lay ahead. In both cases I felt surrounded in love and affirmed in my role as leader.

The scriptures make it clear that through baptism all believers are called and commissioned to proclaim the good news of Jesus. In Peter's first letter we read, "You, however, are 'a chosen race, a royal priesthood, a holy nation, a people he claims for his own to proclaim the glorious works' of the One who called you from darkness into his marvelous light" (1 Pt 2:9). To give order to that Christian calling, there was always a need for Christian leaders. These roles of leadership developed and differentiated as the church grew. What is evident in all the roles of leadership in the New Testament is that they are roles of *service* for the good of the community. Paul expressed that very well when he wrote, "It is he (Christ) who gave apostles, prophets, evangelists, pastors and teachers in roles of service for the faithful to build up the body of Christ" (Eph 4:11-12). Another translation of that verse tells us that Christian leaders are to "equip the saints for the work of ministry." As servants, the leaders are called to enable all the baptized to minister according to their spiritual gifts, to equip them with the skills which they need to minister according to their baptismal calling.

Paul had come to realize in his lifetime that leadership, as Jesus had established it, was a ministry of service. He regarded himself as a "servant of Christ and administrator of the mysteries of God" (1 Cor 4:1). Like him,

Christian leaders may not always understand the power and mystery of the words and sacraments which they minister, but they are commissioned to administer them faithfully as servants of Christ. The sacrament of holy orders developed as a way of allowing those called in such roles of service to experience the encouragement, support and protection of Christ and the community. Jesus' prayer for his apostles before his death indicated his desire to bless and protect all Christian leaders.

In light of all the scripture passages regarding Christian leadership, it is somewhat disappointing that the church eventually limited the sacrament of holy orders to the three offices of bishop, priest and deacon, and to men only. The New Testament gives evidence that when new forms of leadership were necessary, such forms were created and those serving in them were affirmed and supported through prayers and the laying on of hands. While the fact that Jesus chose only men as apostles could be a basis for limiting some roles of leadership to men, it does not exclude numerous positions of leadership from being shared by all. There are many and varied leadership roles within the Christian community in which the sacrament of ordination could be a powerful experience of the community's encouragement as well as the Lord's support and protection. It could be an expression of affirmation and empowerment in Jesus' name for all those who "equip the saints for the work of ministry."

The scriptures give evidence that Jesus saw the need for training leaders to carry on his mission. By his example and words he enabled his apostles and other disciples to teach and minister in his name. His words and witness told them that they were to be servant-leaders, and his prayer for them before he died told them that he would always be there to protect and guide them on their way. As the needs of the church grew in number and diversity, the apostles commissioned or "ordained" others to carry on the work of the Lord. The offices of presbyter-bishop and deacon emerged as the primary leadership positions affirmed by prayers and the laying on of hands, and called to give order and encouragement to the gifts of all the baptized. It was through the enabling of the gifts within the communities by the leaders, in unity with the mission of the universal church, that Christianity grew.

Historical Development

Leadership positions in New Testament times seemed to be based on the personal holiness of the leader. We read that in choosing the first deacons, the apostles looked for seven men "acknowledged to be deeply spiritual and prudent" (Acts 6:3), and Barnabas, who was selected to care for the community of Antioch, is described as "a good man filled with the Holy Spirit and faith" (Acts 11:24). When Paul instructed Timothy and Titus as to what qualities to look for in selecting presbyter-bishops and deacons, he described attributes which indicate a deep personal spirituality. Already in the second century there was a movement away from focusing on the personal spirituality of the leaders to accenting their role or function. This movement led to more emphasis on the power of ordination and less stress on the power of personal holiness or oneness with the Lord.

There is evidence that during this century the presbyter-bishops became the exclusive leaders of the community celebrations of the Eucharist. As the celebration of the Eucharist became less of a community meal and more of a ritual, it took on characteristics of the Old Testament Jewish sacrifices and consequently the presbyter-bishops who led those rituals came to be described with terms borrowed from the Jewish priesthood of the Old Testament. They were seen more as performers of rituals than ministers of the presence of Christ.

This association of the Christian ordained leaders with the Old Testament priesthood led the church in the West to request priests and bishops to abstain from sexual intercourse as the Old Testament priests had done for reasons of ritual purity. This request for voluntary celibacy was in part the basis for celibacy being made mandatory for priests and bishops in 1139. It is also part of what led to a class distinction between the "hierarchy" who were ordained and the "laity" who were not. While it is appropriate to have respect for leaders, this class distinction finds no basis in the ministry of Jesus.

By the third century the church had established the office of presbyter or priest as distinct from the bishop. As the communities grew in size, one person was not able to take care of all the ministry needs. Bishops continued to function as the primary teachers and overseers. They were responsible for protecting the communities from false teachers and prophets as well as keeping communities in unity with the larger church. Priests functioned as extensions of their bishops with a certain autonomy to set policies for the communities they served and to lead them in worship. Deacons functioned as helpers of the bishop, totally dependent on their bishops for their authority.

History shows us that bishops during the third century were elected by the people, but they were ordained by other bishops. After 312 when Christianity became the official religion of the Roman Empire, the bishops became very influential and their involvement in civil affairs increased. During that century bishops began choosing other bishops. In the fourth and fifth centuries they took on more of a ceremonial role in the community celebration of the Eucharist, presiding in a fashion much like the Jewish high priest of the Old Testament.

During the fifth century priests grew in their autonomy as they were sent out to care for the new communities arising in the rural areas. While the priests were always seen as extensions of the bishops, they had to make more and more of their own decisions as they traveled farther and farther from the central community led by the bishop. Eventually they took up residence in these new communities, guiding them in accord with the directives of the bishop. As we saw in our examination of the Eucharist, there was at this time a strong sense of unity between the bishop and his priests. The number of priests increased during this period while the number of deacons declined and remained almost nonexistent until the restoration of the diaconate after the Second Vatican Council.

It is significant to keep in mind that in these early centuries of the church there were many positions of ministry and leadership shared by numerous members of the community. There is evidence, as noted earlier, that many people took the Eucharist home to friends and relatives, and anointed the sick with oil blessed by the bishop. We saw as well that at times a nonordained Christian was the minister of the reconciling love of Jesus and the community. In addition to these, there is evidence that the orders of exorcist, lector, acolyte and porter were not limited to ordained leaders, but were shared in by all the baptized according to their gifts. By the 12th century all of these ministries had become the exclusive right of those who were ordained. It is in recognition of the original practices and the scriptural roots of ministry that the Catholic church has begun affirming again the ministerial gifts of all baptized people.

From the sixth to the eighth centuries there is evidence of much missionary activity going on and numerous priests being ordained for ministry. It was also during this time that the spiritual power of bishops and priests became more and more fused with royal power. Bishops were involved in the political developments of the time, and priests' loyalties were being divided between the Lord whom they served and the feudal lord who often selected them for their office. A classic example of this intermingling of royalty and spiritual leadership was the crowning of Charlemagne as Emperor of Rome by Pope Leo III in 800. The roles of bishops and priests were developing into positions of power with less and less emphasis on the servant role of Christian leadership.

During the 11th century Pope Gregory VII sought to reform the church leadership by making the papacy a stronger and more authoritative position. This was at a time when the Eastern Catholic church centered in Constantinople had just split from the Western Catholic church centered in Rome. Part of the reason for that split was that the papacy had moved from being a position of honored leadership in the early centuries of the church to being a position of authoritative leadership, and the leaders of the Eastern church did not feel obligated to comply with all the rules of the Roman pope. The strengthening of the papacy only widened the split. In recent years through understanding and reconciliation, the hurts and alienation caused by this split have to a large extent been healed.

As we have seen, the seven sacraments were officially named as such in the 12th century, and by that time most of them were administered by a priest or bishop. The sacrament of holy orders in this setting came to be understood as an investment of power to an individual, separate from their leadership role in a community. Since receiving the sacrament of ordination at that time did not require much training at all, many men received this "power" and then traveled around making money administering the other sacraments. Part of the reforms of the 16th century made seminary training and spiritual formation a requirement for this sacrament in order to stop such abuses.

In 1139 celibacy was officially made mandatory for bishops and priests, though there is evidence that it was not universally observed following this regulation. There was no theological explanation given for the law. While, as noted before, celibacy was requested of bishops and priests at one time in history, this mandatory law seems to stem from the strong negativity toward secularism and women during the period, as well as a disciplinary measure against those bishops and priests who were passing on their wealth to their children. Later theologians began to find spiritual meaning in celibacy as a way of identifying more closely with Jesus' celibate lifestyle and as a sign of the final resurrection where people "neither marry nor are given in marriage" (Mt 22:30). Jesus did speak of celibacy as an ideal for those who were able to bear it (Mt 19:12), but he never demanded or even asked it of his followers.

In my dealings with priests I find that many of them experience celibacy as a discipline forced upon them if they wish to serve the church in ordained leadership. The acceptance of that discipline out of a deep desire to minister can be a powerful sign of commitment and dedication, but it can also be a source of anger and hurt that colors the words and attitudes of church leaders.

The 13th to 15th centuries saw a decline in the spiritual ministry of church leaders and an overall neglect of the sacraments. The church as a whole went through a real crisis at this time. Even the papacy was split from 1378-1417, with two and for a time three bishops claiming themselves as the "true" pope. Eventually this situation was resolved but the whole church was in need of renewal and reform. The human weaknesses of church leaders during this period were very evident. The ordained leaders had developed their own distinct "clerical world," which had little resemblance to the example of Jesus' ministry. Despite such human errors, the Spirit of Jesus continued to guide the church, calling it back to the one who had called it forth.

The need for reforming the church and the sacraments was evident by the 16th century. The reformers of this century, as we have seen, questioned many of the practices regarding all the sacraments. In reference to the sacrament of holy orders, the reformers denied the legitimacy of papal power and authority over all Christians and they could not agree with priests being ordained primarily and almost exclusively as performers of rituals. Their objections did not bring changes in these two areas, but they did lead the church to establish seminaries to train priests and put more emphasis on priestly spirituality. These differences regarding the authority of the pope and the definition of "valid" priesthood became a major source of division and even hostility between various church denominations through the next centuries. These issues remain the biggest roadblocks to Christian unity today. Recently, however, dialogue over these issues has brought about some reconciliation and a movement toward a mutual respect of the various leadership forms within Christian denominations.

The Second Vatican Council (1962-1965) set the stage for greater Christian unity and a broader vision of ministry. It did this by restoring the structures of its leadership to a more scriptural model, as well as renewing the sacraments according to their scriptural origins. Church leaders began emphasizing the gifts and ministries of all baptized members and speaking of the roles of leadership as roles of service and ministry rather than power. The universal leadership of the church began to be defined not so much as the "power" of the pope, but as the shared authority of the college of bishops under the guidance of the Holy Spirit. The role of the priest came to be understood not so much as the performer of rituals, but as one who coordinates the ministries within a community and enables the "saints" to use their gifts for service. The office of deacon was restored to its original design and all baptized were encouraged to participate in many of the ministries which they had done in the earlier days of the church. Though these changes are not all complete, they represent a major renewal in the Catholic church and a sign of the power and guidance of the Holy Spirit.

I have to admit that I struggled to watch the church change as I went through my years of seminary training. The priesthood to which I aspired in 1965 was not the priesthood to which I was ordained in 1977. I did not like to see so much of the old being taken away at the time, yet I now recognize the great blessings that the renewal in the church has brought about. I distinctly remember the wise words of one of our priest-teachers during those years of change. He said, "Remember, you are committing your life to Christ as his servant, not to a form of priesthood that may not be around when you are ordained." His words came true and it is my commitment to the Lord that keeps me in love with his church and the form of ministry to which he has called me.

As I reflect on the priesthood of the future, I see a need for further changes, changes that evolve from a deep inner desire to be *servants of Christ* empowered by the strength flowing from his love. Even while we wait for future developments and changes we must recognize that the real power of Christian ministry comes from personal holiness, personal submission to the true Servant-Leader. Some of these developments or changes may come about only through forgiveness of past hurts and inner healing of present wounds. This is particularly true concerning the issue of women and men in positions of Christian leadership and ministry.

It is revealing and disheartening that much of the language used by women seeking ordination conveys a desire for power and control rather than service. It is equally revealing and disheartening that many of the words used by the leaders of the church to justify an all-male clergy convey an insecurity, fear and struggle to continue positions of power. Such underlying tones reveal much inner pain and lead me to believe that men and women of leadership in the church are not so much seeking a theological resolution of that issue as they are searching for inner healing of their wounds regarding their sexuality, and the ways in which that gift can be used as a means of God's grace. It is the unforgiven sin and the unhealed wounds dealt to men and women in the past and still being inflicted today that are in need of understanding, reconciliation and healing by Christ's love ministered through the care of one another. Neither theological answers nor additional verbal weapons on the part of anyone will bring resolution of the real issues. The search for truth in this matter includes an openness to honest self-examination, sincere reconciliation, and the desire for inner healing.

This issue may have been complicated by the fact that the men responsible for addressing it have been forced to live a celibate lifestyle. While I recognize the powerful witness of dedication that this style of life can be, it has at times caused a fear of sexuality and a repression of loneliness that makes it hard for priests and bishops to consider or affirm the gifts and callings of women and married men in the church. The letting go of "privileges of ministry" or "positions of honor and power" once relegated exclusively to bishops and priests, can be a real source of pain to a man whose only "children" are his ministry and his community. These issues are not so much theological as they are emotional, needing the healing power of love.

Throughout all its developments holy orders has remained a necessary and life-giving sacrament. It has its roots in the affirming words of Jesus to his apostles and the witness of his servant leadership. His followers have sought in their own human ways to preserve his attitude toward leadership and to affirm those who feel called to serve as leaders. History tells us that this journey has not always been easy or without error, but it has always had the guidance of the Holy Spirit. I believe that the Lord has poured out a new portion of his Spirit upon the church in recent years bringing about the renewal mentioned in these pages. I trust that this same Spirit will guide the church in the future to new growth and a deeper unity with its Creator.

EPILOGUE

Jesus left us his precious words, his unique attitudes, his powerful example. His followers recorded his words, proclaimed his attitudes, and repeated his gestures in order that others might encounter the power of his risen presence. We have looked at these encounters, these sacraments, these special ways in which the saving grace of Christ can be experienced. They are not magic; they are not always predictable. They are occasions, privileges, opportunities for us to be immersed in the presence of Christ through words and actions. They are gifts originating with Jesus, molded and fashioned by those who have gone before us in faith, and given personality by those committed to celebrating the saving mysteries of God's love. Despite the errors of history and the differences of opinion regarding their effects, the sacraments remain gifts of love, gifts of life from the giver of all life.

I continue to marvel at the power of Christ's sacraments. I am amazed at the many ways he touches the lives of people through these encounters, these holy mysteries. I rejoice that the church continues to probe these mysteries seeking to make them ever richer experiences of the Lord's love. I am thankful to those who "lay down their lives" to make these sacraments true encounters with the risen Lord.

My hope is that this journey into the past has shed some new light for you on the wonder of the sacraments. I hope it has answered questions that keep you from experiencing the Lord's love. I hope this journey is only the first of many more journeys into the mystery of God's love among us. I pray that it will help all of us as growing

Christians to take future steps toward discovering the true
essence and origin of all sacraments — Jesus Christ.

> Jesus said,
>
> "I solemnly assure you,
>
> the man who has faith in me
> will do the works I do,
> and greater far than these.
> Why? Because I go to the Father,
> and whatever you ask in my name I will do,
> so as to glorify the Father in the Son"
>   (Jn 14:12-13).

HELPFUL READING

(Books that deal with all seven sacraments.)

Bausch, William. *A New Look at the Sacraments.* Mystic, CT: Twenty-third Publications. 1983. (A pastoral treatment of the sacraments as they developed and exist today.)

Cooke, Bernard. *Sacraments and Sacramentality.* Mystic, CT: Twenty-third Publications. 1983. (A theological treatment of what sacrament means.)

Documents of Vatican II. New York: Guild Press. 1966. (Contains the 16 documents resulting from the discussions and decisions of the Second Vatican Council, 1962-1965.)

Martos, Joseph. *Doors to the Sacred.* New York: Doubleday. 1981. (An in-depth study of the historical development of the sacraments.)

McBrien, Richard. *Catholicism.* Minneapolis, MN: Winston Press. 1980. (A valuable reference book containing concise articles on the sacraments and numerous articles on the history and teachings of the Catholic church.)

New Catholic Encyclopedia. New York: McGraw-Hill. 1967. (Contains detailed articles on each of the sacraments.)

Rahner, Karl. *The Church and the Sacraments.* New York: Herder and Herder. 1963. (Gives a theological understanding of sacraments and their relationship to the whole church.)

Scanlan, T.O.R., Michael and Ann Therese Shields, R.S.M. *And Their Eyes Were Opened.* Ann Arbor, MI: Servant Books. 1976. (An easy-to-read book focusing on the life-giving power of the sacraments.)

Schillebeeckx, O.P., Edward. *Christ, the Sacrament of the Encounter with God.* New York: Sheed and Ward. 1963. (A classic theological work on the meaning of sacrament.)

(Books that deal with an individual sacrament.)

Baptism - Confirmation

Brockett, R.S.C.J., Lorna. *Theology of Baptism.* Notre Dame, IN: Fides. 1971. (Contains a simple history of the sacrament of baptism.)

Kiesling, O.P., Christopher. *Confirmation and Full Life in the Spirit.* Cincinnati, OH: St. Anthony Messenger Press. 1973. (Gives an understanding of the sacrament of confirmation and its relationship to living in an awareness of God's Spirit.)

Eucharist

Powers, Joseph. *The Eucharist.* New York: Herder and Herder. 1967. (Gives a history and theological understanding of the sacrament of the Eucharist.)

Schillebeeckx, O.P., Edward. *The Eucharist.* New York: Sheed and Ward. 1968. (A theological treatment of the meaning of Eucharist.)

Reconciliation

The Mystery of Sin and Forgiveness. Michael Taylor, S.J. (editor). New York: Alba House. 1971. (Contains numerous articles on the theology and history of the sacrament of reconciliation.)

Anointing of the Sick

Kelsey, Morton. *Healing and Christianity.* New York: Harper & Row. 1973. (An in-depth history of the Christian healing ministry.)

Shlemon, Barbara: Dennis and Matthew Linn, S.J. *To Heal as Jesus Healed.* Notre Dame, IN: Ave Maria Press. 1978. (A simple, personal book on the power of healing and the sacrament of anointing.)

Marriage

Schillebeeckx, O.P., Edward. *Marriage: Human Reality and Saving Mystery.* New York: Sheed & Ward. 1965. (An in-depth treatment of the Old and New Testament roots of the sacrament of marriage.)

Holy Orders

Brown, S.S., Raymond. *Priest and Bishop — Biblical Reflections.* New York: Paulist Press. 1970. (A scholarly treatment of the early roots of the sacrament of holy orders.)

Rahner, Karl. *Servants of the Lord.* New York: Herder and Herder. 1968. (Reflections of this scholarly priest on the servant role of priesthood.)